F.A.T.E.

FROM AUTHORS TO ENTREPRENEURS:
THE PERSONAL SIDE OF INDIE PUBLISHING

STEPHANIE CASHER
JAMES W. LEWIS
OMAR LUQMAAN-HARRIS

**TPC
BOOKS**

THE PANTHEON COLLECTIVE (TPC)
www.pantheoncollective.com

The Pantheon Collective (TPC)
P.O. Box 799
Santa Cruz, CA 95061

FATE: From Authors to Entrepreneurs – The Personal Side of
Indie Publishing. Copyright © 2013 by TPC Books

ISBN: 978-0-9827193-8-1 (Paperback)
ISBN: 978-0-9827193-9-8 (Ebook)

Printed in United States of America

Cover: Designed by Creativindie Covers
Interior: Designed by Stephanie Casher

To the Family, Friends, and Fans who have supported us along the way.

Dear Author,

If you are like us, you have spent countless years honing your craft as a writer, learning about the publishing business, querying agents, and dreaming of seeing your work on both online and physical bookshelves. Chances are you've collected your fair share of rejection letters from literary agents as well. We definitely feel your pain! Back in 2009, we were on the same path until the three of us joined forces and started a publishing company. Now, four years later, we have successfully published four bestselling, award-winning novels, sold thousands of copies of each book, and almost 30,000 copies total.

Our mission for doing all this, however, was never solely about accolades and sales. We also wanted to blaze a trail so that you, and authors like you, could avoid our missteps and elevate the independent publishing field even higher. *F.A.T.E.* is ultimately about finding inspiration in our struggle and taking away our best practices so that you can take control of your own publishing destiny, just as we did.

This is not a self-help book in the traditional sense. Nor is it a "how-to" primer. We want you to know that from the outset. This is a story of three driven individuals with a shared dream coming together to become greater than the sum of their parts. There are many paths to the publishing Promised Land; this just happens to be ours.

PROLOGUE:

Three Author's Journeys

James

My "birth write" (pun intended) started with me doing the usual as a pre-teen—getting in trouble. As punishment, my mother sentenced me to house confinement. Not only that, she decided to try something different: She made me write a story every night for a week. I was like, "What 'chu talkin' 'bout, Willis?"

Well, they don't say, "Moms know best" for nothing. I had no idea this unique form of torture would plant a passion in me that refuses to fade, even now that I'm a grown-ass man. Initially, I didn't use my newfound "penmanship" to become a full-blown writer, though. Oh, no. I became what every young man wanted to be back in da high-top fade 80's—a rapper.

MC Juicy J was born! I figured I had the "juice" to bust rhymes (we don't say "juice" anymore; we use "swag" today). I also convinced myself that my rhymes were so juicy my name should reflect my skills! The name Juicy J was perfect (as silly as "Juicy J" sounds, an award-winning rapper today uses the same name)! And with my fellow partners-in-rhyme, MC Dazzy D and DJ RMC, we became … who else?

The Three Bad Rockers.

Fresh new Pumas, fat shoelaces, and bomber jackets sealed the deal for rap superstardom. We sounded pretty good, considering our hand-me-down equipment and my—

and I've finally come to terms with this—third-grade lyrical flow. But I give props to our adolescent creativity. Of course, my rap star delusion ended shortly after I graduated from high school. Then I joined the Navy and the pen stopped. I didn't write anything creative for the next ten years.

The Internet brought the pen back.

In 1999 I found a site called Timbooktu.com, a forum where aspiring writers can post short stories and poetry. I became a frequent visitor, reading all the stories. The more I read, the more my juices stirred. No, not the juices that birthed MC Juicy J (thankfully), but the kind that made me a writer again—just like that little boy who Mom had enslaved at the kitchen table almost twenty years before.

I wrote a short erotica story about a woman's comical experience during a one-night stand and posted it online (this story would later become my second novel *A Hard Man is Good to Find*). Of course, I was all proud and stuff; even told my mom about it. Then something completely unexpected happened: I received feedback. The day after posting my story, three people emailed to say they really liked it. Let me tell you, nothing feels better than when someone enjoys your work. I was in demand!

So I wrote another story called *Educating the Ignorant* and found other places to publish it online. The floodgates opened shortly after. I received emails not only from people in this country, but from I'd-only-seen-on-a-map places like Britain, South Africa, and Australia. International demand! I was hooked!

I kept writing stories and eventually personal essays and articles. I immersed myself in the craft and business of writing. I even attended writer's conferences and joined writer's groups. Gradually, I built a nice list of publication credits, ones I could proudly write on query letters for editors and literary agents.

Then I wrote another short story that received even more attention. I wrote it from a woman's point of view. It had adult content, so I pitched it to an editor at an erotica site. The editor loved it and posted it online.

Man! A tsunami of feedback followed. I received an average of two emails a day for at least four months, all of them praising my story with words like "extremely funny," "best short story I ever read," and "gifted." Beautiful thing. Time to look past molehills and climb mountains, so I started a novel.

I finished the novel in 2002. Prouder than a father with the last name Manning, I fantasized of big-time author riches. Within seven years, I sent queries, got an agent, lost that agent, then found another one. I told myself if I didn't have a book deal by my military retirement in September 2009, I'd give self-publishing a shot.

Well, retirement rolled around and no book deal. Just countless rejections. I'm a man of my word, so I decided to open my mind to the idea of self-publishing. I wasn't sure how to get started, but luckily, my fellow pillars of Pantheon helped blaze the path. The partnership made sense. We each have unique strengths and the drive to make it happen. No egos, no power trips, no lead singer in this group. Just three writers sharing ideas and helping each other fortify their dreams.

With my partners riding this road beside me, I don't plan on stopping anytime soon—unless the Rap Gods come calling again. Naw, just kidding. I'll just stick with books and leave Juicy J in the shower. Nobody raps better in there.

Omar

I started *One Blood* in January 2000 (back then I was calling it *Simmons Park*) in my final year as an MBA student at Florida A&M University in Tallahassee, FL. The world was a different place back then but already changing. George Bush had just been elected President in a controversial election and there was this feeling among many that something bad was going to happen. Eighteen months later, the Twin Towers fell.

During that time, I moved from Tallahassee to Sao Paulo, Brazil, where I lived and worked from May 2000 until August 2001. I didn't get much writing done while living in Brazil, I must admit, but the poverty and inequality I saw there definitely resonated and would manifest in my writing years later. I returned to the States a month before 9/11— a watershed event that got me focused and writing again. I started making real progress on my first draft.

Six months later, after writing myself into a corner, I put the manuscript down for some time. I graduated with my MBA in May 2002 and started working in Philadelphia.

I was very inspired to be living in the city that birthed DJ Jazzy Jeff and the Fresh Prince, The Roots, Jill Scott, and many others. I was performing spoken word at spots all over town and writing quite a bit when I wasn't working or performing. My story kept changing and evolving, so I decided to start over and rebuild the story from the characters outward, instead of from the plot inward. The novel morphed from *Simmons Park* (a story of trying to make up for past actions) into *Bad Blood* (a story of two warring families).

Over the next four years, I poured my heart and soul into the manuscript, and in May 2006 (eight months after Hurricane Katrina) I reached THE END for the first time. Certain I had a masterpiece on my hands (an unedited, 600 page, 180,000 word masterpiece—but a masterpiece no less), I immediately began investigating literary agents to whom I could pitch to get the book sold. This search led me to the Black Writer's Reunion and Conference in Dallas, TX—a decision that would prove to be one of the most fortuitous of my life. While there, I got a brief taste of success when the literary agent I pitched (badly) requested my whole manuscript! I was sure I was on my way.

I also met two people at the conference who would greatly help me on my publishing journey—Stephanie Casher and Michelle Chester. Michelle agreed to copyedit my manuscript in a completely unreasonable two-week time frame. After receiving her edits and making the changes, I submitted the manuscript to the literary agent. I also sent it out to eight or so advance readers to get their feedback. And they all loved it!

In August 2006, I moved back to Sao Paulo. While waiting to hear back from the literary agent, I started writing my second novel, *The Uneasy Sleep of Giants*. In October I got the notice that the agent was passing on my manuscript. Never one to be derailed by a setback, I took the feedback from my advance readers and went back in to *Bad Blood* to make some tweaks.

It took me another seven months or so to get through the manuscript again as my day job was kicking my ass! In May 2007, I flew back to the U.S. for work and linked up with Stephanie and her beau, James W. Lewis (an author as well), in NYC and we had a fateful dinner at Bubba Gump Shrimp Co. in Times Square. We made a pact that if the three of us hadn't succeeded in landing a book deal by the end of 2009, we'd publish ourselves. None of us believed that was even a remote possibility...there was no way we wouldn't be published in two and a half years...

So, two and a half years later, LOL, I was sitting in Barnes & Noble in Hoboken, NJ (I'd moved back to the States in October 2008), working my way through yet another rewrite of the novel that had evolved from *Bad Blood* to *One Blood* after *Bad Blood* received 17 rejections from literary agents (too long, too confusing, too different) and some very hard to swallow feedback from Stephanie and professional manuscript consultant, Anita Diggs (poor characterization, poor pacing).

Barack Obama was celebrating the one-year anniversary of his amazing election and I was feeling very "Yes You Can-ish." I picked up my cell to compose a life-changing text...

Stephanie

I started writing my first novel as therapy. I've written in my journal pretty much every day since the 7th grade, and throughout adolescence, I constantly searched for new and interesting ways to express myself. My attempt at penning a romance novel was really just an experiment birthed out of boredom, never meant to be serious. I was shocked when friends and family members responded favorably to the work in progress.

"This is really good!"
"This could be published!"

Really? Maybe I'm on to something here…

I finished the first draft of my first novel in November 2005, and was so proud of myself. I mean, wow, I wrote a book! How many people can tack that onto their list of accomplishments? Armed with my completed manuscript, I set out to learn as much as I could about the publishing business. I attended writer's workshops and panels, read up on industry news, and identified who the "players" were. I learned about queries and agents and the proper way to format a manuscript. I hit the conference circuit to further expand my network, communing with other writers, pitching to editors and agents, and generating genuine interest in my book. Soon I had over a dozen partials and full manuscripts under consideration. It was so validating to get that kind of response from industry professionals, and with each request, I became more convinced that this was indeed what I was supposed to be doing with my life.

I turned thirty in 2006, and as many of you know, the transition from your twenties to thirties prompts all kinds of meditation and soul-searching. The more I thought about it, the more dissatisfied I felt in my day job. There had to be more than punching a clock, right? I must have a greater calling in life... In the throes of my Saturn Return, I was determined to clarify my life path and rechart my course.

Part of my new commitment to pursuing a passionate existence was the decision to take five weeks off in the summer of 2006 and drive across the country. A cross-country road trip was something I'd ALWAYS wanted to do, but I could never find the time or money or right companion. But that summer, I decided, no more excuses—I'm going to make this happen. So on July 7, 2006 I packed up my trusty Toyota and hit the road.

I knew this journey would be a turning point in my life, but I never could have imagined how significant that summer would turn out to be.

On July 12th, I arrived in Dallas. The plan was to visit with my cousin Doug for a couple of days and attend the Black Writer's Reunion and Conference (BWRC). It was here that I met James and Omar for the first time. Omar and I bonded instantly, anointing each other "Kindred" after only a few moments acquaintance. And James, well, James ended up being a pretty significant part of my life as well.

Needless to say, after the BWRC, I was incredibly energized. I had reputable editors and agents interested in seeing the FULL manuscript, and I was beginning to act and feel like a real writer. I knew it was only a matter of time before I got a break.

As any writer will tell you, there's a lot of waiting in this business. Write, Submit, Wait; Wash, Rinse, Repeat. Before you know it years have passed. As 2009 drew to a close, I started to feel frustrated that I had a product people actually wanted to read, but I couldn't deliver the goods.

I started to mull over self-publishing. After some extensive web research, I discovered that outfits like Lulu and CreateSpace had made it relatively easy to get your book out. Technology really has come a long way and the DIY (Do It Yourself) route is incredibly cost-effective. After weighing all my options, I decided to go ahead and self-publish *When Love Isn't Enough*.

Once I committed to this path, I couldn't believe how quickly things started to get off the ground. The proverbial stars aligned, and the pieces started falling into place. Ideas and inspiration were coming fast and furious. I wondered if it might be feasible for me to go ahead and start my own publishing company. I've always been an independent woman, a "Boss Lady" if you will, and the entrepreneurial path appealed to me. As I debated the pros and cons of print-on-demand (POD) vs. starting my own company, I received a serendipitous text from my Kindred Omar, apparently in the midst of some meditations of his own...

F.A.T.E.

1: A Serendipitous Text

Omar

It was a Saturday afternoon. I had committed to finally finishing the new ending to my first novel, *One Blood*, about a supernatural curse tormenting a group of people unaware of their hidden connections. The words were coming fast and furious, for once. I could see the finish line.

Then a thought stabbed me in the brain like a massive charley horse: *What the hell is the point of this?*

I looked around. I was surrounded by published work. Would Qwantu Amaru's (my pen name) work ever ascend into this Pantheon? At the rate I was going, maybe sometime before the world ended in 2012. Maybe.

Getting published is a long, arduous process. Finish the first draft. Revise. Content edit. Revise. Copyedit. Revise. Write the query letter. Submit to agents. Collect rejections. Revise query and send out again. Collect rejections. Revise manuscript based on agent's suggestions. Continue to pitch and submit. Collect more rejections. Revise again. A pattern emerges. Finally catch the interest of an editor. Editor fights with other editors until they agree to publish your book. Editors then fight with the sales and marketing team until they agree on the best way to get your book into bookstores. Get a launch date. Choose book cover. Write back cover copy. Get early reviews. Build buzz. The book comes out!

And if you're exceptionally fortunate, your book sells just enough copies to allow you to keep your contract and make 1-2 percent royalties on a novel it took you six years to complete, three years to edit, one year to sell to an editor, and another eighteen months to actually see on a bookshelf.

This shit is for the birds, I thought. I was 32-years-old. My day job as a successful marketing executive was on its last legs—at least at the company that had groomed me for the past seven years. They'd been bought out by a bigger company. No room for someone like me. On to the next one.

But writing was still there. Writing had been my savior ever since I wrote my first poem twelve years earlier. I desperately needed it to save me from an uncertain future. But to do this I needed to regain some control over the process.

I picked up my iPhone and found the contact info for Stephanie Casher, a fellow author in the struggle and an exceptional editor who was half the reason my book was nearly finished. One thought put a smile on my face and hope in my heart. What if she and I, and her writer boyfriend, James Lewis, joined forces to start our own publishing company?

And so I wrote the most important text message of my life.

2: The Proverbial Stars Align

Stephanie
Receiving Omar's text was one of the most serendipitous things that has ever happened to me. Serendipitous because I had already made the decision, three weeks prior, to self-publish my novel *When Love Isn't Enough*. I had even gone so far as to select a Print on Demand (POD) service and hire a photographer to shoot the cover image. So it took me all of two minutes to reply back with an emphatic "YES!!!"

Completing a novel is a major accomplishment; many writers never get to that point. I've often heard that starting a novel is easy—finishing it is the hard part. Well, after five years of shopping my manuscript around, I discovered that finishing a novel is not the hardest part of this process. The hardest part, in my opinion, is all the hustling and heartache that goes into the process of *selling* the manuscript.

As Omar said, it's always been tough to break into the publishing business. Like many industries, the publishing industry is dominated by an elite group of what I refer to as "Big Dogs," and getting the attention of a Big Dog without the representation of an agent is damn near impossible. However, getting the attention of an agent proved to be just as difficult. As with anything, advancement in this business often comes down to who you know. But how does one become known when folks are reluctant to take a chance on someone unknown?

This shit really *was* for the birds.

Omar and I have always considered ourselves Kindred, and it doesn't surprise me that we came to the same "Aha" moment at the exact same time. And joining forces to start a publishing company sounded like a great idea. I intuitively knew that what we could accomplish together would be so much greater than what either of us could accomplish on our own. The only question was, could we get James to come on board?

3: Working Together: Smart, Crazy, or Just Plain Dumb?

James

Hell-to-the-naw.

That was my initial reply when Stephanie proposed the idea of starting a publishing venture with her and Omar. That response stemmed from a hardcore belief of mine: Don't ever go into business with friends or family. You want the quickest way to end a strong relationship? Start a business together. Why do you think groups like NWA broke up? Yeah, things start off with a hunky-dory-everything's-beautiful-I-love-you-man vibe, but once you mix egos, money, and friendship, friends become like Eazy E against Dr. Dre.

In 2009, I went through a major life readjustment which included military retirement, short-selling my beloved first home, moving from Southern California to Northern California, cohabiting with Stephanie, and going back to college at 38-years-old. Stephanie helped facilitate these transitions with sound advice, handling the shipment of my household items, and general I-got-your-back-babe support. In a sense, we worked well together already, but I overlooked that small fact. I still viewed mixing business with pleasure as taboo.

Now that I was retired, I had the flexibility to follow all my dreams, including becoming a full-time author. Since I already had a literary agent (my second), I assumed I would have at least two books in Barnes & Noble by retirement, even working on a third. As of September 2009, guess how many of my books were on the shelves? Can you say "zilch?"

I'd told myself if Random House or Kensington hadn't picked up a brother by the time I said "anchors away" to the Navy, I'd give self-publishing a look-see. It appeared my true opportunity at book publication came in Omar's text.

But how could I get past that self-imposed brick wall? Well, I finally saw the big picture...the proverbial "light," if you will. When I delved deeper into the possibilities, I realized we had all the key elements for success—with Omar as the Fortune 500 marketing don; Stephanie as the detailed-oriented, one-woman quality control department; and me as the resource gathering, seasoned veteran, I saw us as a literary Voltron. The Three Musketeers of the written word—a tripod.

I finally told myself, "Screw it. Why not try it, J-Willy?"

So, after many inner battles, J-Willy joined the small "scribe tribe" and stepped one foot onto the unknown path. To my surprise, I was amped up like a hype man for Jay-Z.

But I still had one question that nagged me: How the hell were we gonna pull this off?

4: The 1st Power Summit
December 13, 2009

Once everyone was fully on board, we decided that we really needed a face-to-face meeting to hammer out some of the details. Serendipitously (as will become a recurring theme in this venture), shortly after James made the decision to go "all in" with the company, Omar informed us that he had to fly out to the Bay Area for a job interview. He arranged to arrive a day early so that he could come down to Santa Cruz for our very first Power Summit.

One of the greatest challenges we have as business partners is how to build the foundation for a company when partners are located on two separate coasts. Email, the internet, and web conferencing certainly help to bridge the distance, but nothing compares to the energy generated from three bright minds sitting in a room together, tossing ideas around, in a good ole fashioned face-to-face brainstorming session. When you're contemplating an endeavor of this magnitude, one that will require a significant investment of time *and* money, you need to look people in the eye and know where they're coming from. You need to confirm that you are all on the same page.

The First Power Summit accomplished all that, and more.

5: *The Element of Fate*

Omar

I once blogged about the Illusion of Choice, exploring the idea of why we do what we do and how we end up where we end up. We don't choose our families, where and under what conditions we grow up. But our upbringing has a significant impact on how we live our lives. We don't choose our genetic make-up either. But whether we have a superfast metabolism, bad ticker, or aptitude for foreign languages also has a significant bearing on our existence.

I didn't *choose* to send that text message to Stephanie. My entire life brought me to that moment. It was Fate.

So when a Bay Area pharmaceutical company began courting me at the exact moment we were starting up our fledgling enterprise, I saw the hand of Fate once again at work. Just a short month after that first text, I was flown out to San Francisco (with a first class upgrade) for an interview, and James and Steph were there waiting. The First Power Summit was going down!

The moment the three of us began breathing the same air I felt lightheaded by the power of our synergy. It was frightening how well we all fit together. James as the already published/polished author; Stephanie as the editor extraordinaire and web savvy blogger; and me as the back office marketing/sales/business operations guru.

The enthusiasm was contagious. It was more than a perfect match. It was Fate.

But what name could possibly encompass this powerful union? What identity would we use to propel ourselves headlong into the publishing universe?

It was no coincidence that I'd allocated many brain cells to this self-publishing idea for a long time. And nearly four years earlier I'd come up with a name: Pantheon Publishing.

Why Pantheon, you ask? Because ever since I started writing, I began dreaming about the moment of my ascent into the Pantheon of published authors. Tasting that rarified air. It's a special group, not unlike the Pantheon of Greek Gods.

Stephanie and James agreed. We would scale this mountain together and claim our rightful spot up top.

Now a quick Google search will tell you that there is already a Pantheon Books. They publish mostly graphic novels, but we agreed this was still too close for comfort. So we decided to flip it to TPC: The Pantheon Collective.

Who were we? Three indestructible pillars holding our publishing dreams on high. What were we building? A company with a mission of empowering and inspiring (aspiring) authors to pursue their dreams. How were we going to do it? By combining Stephanie's web and editing prowess, James' passion for research and product launch readiness, and my successful business background.

Together, we were well positioned to tackle the laundry list of tasks before us.

We were committed. We had the tools. Now we had to get to work.

6: *Filling in the Blanks*

James

There we were...three minds, three hearts, three souls... primed for the First Power Summit, and J Willy was ready to go! I could see the big picture in high def—our laser bright future a ball of putty that we could mold any way we wanted. When the dynamic trio convened to hash out this whole self-publishing thingy, I felt like an old-school spandex-wearing superhero.

Prior to our first meeting, Omar not only drafted a presentation for the new venture, he dreamed up the perfect name for us: Pantheon. Say it with me: *Pan-the-on.* Sounds kinda nice, right? Has a majestic ring to it: *Pan-the-on.* Cleans your teeth the moment it rolls off your tongue. I was sold.

Omar had also crafted key corporate questions for us to consider: Who are we? What's our mission? How do we sell a gazillion books? Then a blizzard of brain waves scorched the air, ideas bouncing off each other. The more we harmonized the Pantheon melody, the more I felt like finding my own sword and spandex.

First, we had to decide on a book. Only Steph and I had finished products (Omar was still working on *One Blood*). We agreed that promoting one book at a time would be more practical, but which one? *Sellout* or *When Love Isn't Enough*? Well...

Because of my years toiling in the literary game establishing publication credits, my partners decided it made more sense for *Sellout* to go first out the gate. Me. First up to bat on a field of dreams.

I played it cool on the outside, but inside? I was a 12-year-old girl screeching her lungs out. We had just laid the roots of a publishing company, stirring our various skill sets and unique personalities in one big bowl of hot Pantheon soup. This was it! No nickel-and-dime stuff here. Only future dollar signs and bottom lines.

I could see us Amazon-ing our books around the world despite the shaky legs of the industry. We had developed the perfect model to excel. Three minds. One mission. No limits.

So many items on the plate, though, not only to promote *Sellout*, but The Pantheon Collective as a company. The goal was to have *Sellout* ready for the Black Writer's Reunion and Conference in June 2010. That gave us six months, which wasn't a lot of time. It didn't take long for me to realize the clock wouldn't stop for us. The heat was on.

7: The Power of Three

Stephanie
When I first set out on this journey to self-publish, I had planned to do it all by myself. After all, that's been the way I functioned up until very recently. I've never been comfortable relying on other people, asking for help, or accepting help when it was offered. That's just not the Capricorn way.

The first thing we did was set a standing weekly meeting time. As mentioned before, maintaining a bi-coastal partnership means we did not have the luxury of regular, in-person check-ins. Shoot, the time difference alone made scheduling phone dates a challenge. We needed to figure out a remote communication system that would maximize productivity, and get organized.

Thankfully, three minds are better than one, and solutions presented themselves. Invoking the "Power of Three," we divided and conquered. We were each assigned an area and a set of tasks. Steph immediately started a Google Group so we could have a dedicated common space online to upload documents, brainstorm ideas, and post draft blogs. To keep ourselves organized (and accountable), a Master Task List was created, so we could have a clear sense of who was responsible for what, while tracking our progress.

Omar took charge of compiling the weekly agendas in PowerPoint in advance of each meeting, while James crawled the web in research mode, collecting links and information. As the structures were put in place, we began to act and behave as a business, which proved to be both exhilarating and overwhelming.

As the Master Task List began to take shape, it soon became clear that there was *a lot* of work to do, and not a lot of time to do it in. It was time to roll up our sleeves and get to hustlin'!

9: Polishing the Product

Stephanie

At our First Power Summit, after we settled on the name The Pantheon Collective, we came up with this analogy of three pillars, each holding up a side of the company. Each pillar is strong on its own, but without one, the whole structure crumbles. One of the first things we needed to do moving forward was decide which pillar we were, and how we would each hold up our end of the structure.

My unique contribution to the company is my editing skills. I'm one of those freaks who actually *enjoys* the editing process. I willingly subject myself to countless revisions, to endless tinkering and refining. I think I've been through *When Love Isn't Enough* almost a dozen times. I always have my editor's hat on, which is both a blessing and a curse. Since I started editing, I've discovered that I can't even enjoy reading for pleasure anymore, unless the book is extremely well-written. I'm always wanting to correct stuff.

Before we decided to form TPC, I was already editing the work of both my partners. I've also paid to have my work edited by professionals, from whom I learned a great deal. Authors should never be so arrogant as to think they don't need an editor. We are all too close to our work to see what's wrong with it. That second opinion is indispensable, and my primary function within the company is to be the second set of eyes for all the projects we put out.

What this meant was…if we were trying to publish a book in June, I needed to get to work! *Sellout* would need at least two more edits before we could start laying out the book (a content edit, then a copyedit), so I was officially operating within a tight timeframe.

While I have great confidence in my editing skills, I knew that if we were going to launch an independent publishing venture, in order for us to succeed, the product had to be tight. There was absolutely no room for any quality issues that might signify a substandard product. We had to put our best foot forward, and that weight was on *my* shoulders.

To step my game up, I decided to enroll in the Professional Sequence in Editing being offered through UC Berkeley Extension. I had always intended to branch off into freelance editing (if I've got the skills, there's no reason I shouldn't be getting paid for it, lol), so I welcomed the opportunity to acquire the proper training. I just had no idea how challenging it would be to be editing a manuscript, taking a class, starting a company, and working a full-time job, all at the same time. I was taking multi-tasking to a whole other level up in here!

I found myself editing pretty much 24-7. Between *Sellout*, the TPC blog, homework exercises, or reports and correspondence at my day job (where I did a significant amount of writing as well), I was always on the grind. It's a good thing I loved my job.

10: You're My Obsession

James

Obsession: *Domination of thoughts or feelings by a persistent idea, image, or desire.*

I could relate because I had my own obsession: How do we promote The Pantheon Collective and sell a gazillion copies of *Sellout* and books thereafter?

As a full-time college student, I knew I should've been concentrating on the topic at hand, but the professor became the teacher from Charlie Brown and all I heard was, "Mwa, mwa, mwa." I often fantasized about how I could apply my classroom studies to book sales:

In Critical Thinking: How can critical thinking help me sell 5000 copies of *Sellout*?

In Algebra: Will I use the Pythagorean Theorem to sell 5000 copies of Sellout?

En Español: Puedo vender 5000 libros de *Sellout* en seis meses?

So much pressure! We started an American dream, but if we couldn't apply our goals to reality, The Pantheon Collective would become The Pantheon Rejected. And the first item up for bid from The Pantheon Collective come June?

You guessed it—my book, *Sellout*, which had to sell, sell, *sell* to keep us afloat until *When Love Isn't Enough* debuted.

This thought gave me a rush *and* stage fright. Made me talk to myself. Kept me way too focused. Forced me to "unlisten" when my girl said something. Yeah, I needed help!

But I was beyond help. As we drew closer to our scheduled launch, TPC pushed me to work into the wee hours of the night. I couldn't sleep until I finished a blog. I couldn't eat until I posted a new Twitter link. I wouldn't leave the room until I finished another chapter. Back all sore from sitting in a small-ass chair for hours, but I wouldn't budge.

I knew it would get worse. Once *Sellout* launched, my "sickness" would spread into a kind of hardcore addiction anyone on the grind knows about. Only hustlers willing to outwork the next man succeed. When I woke to a new day, the next 18 hours presented more opportunities for our glow to shine brighter, and The Pantheon Collective had to seize them! Why be awake if you can't get your grind on? Everybody hustles in some fashion. Gotta put food on the table and money in your pocket, right? You grind to get that.

But I am still human. Can't forget that, even though I think I'm the black Superman sometimes. I just hoped the pace wouldn't eventually drive me effin' crazy.

11: Getting Down to Business

Omar

I left the First Power Summit with my marching orders firmly in hand. I needed to lay the foundation for our company—the business plan. There is a Portuguese expression that best expressed my feeling in that moment, *frio na barriga*, which literally translates as "cold in the belly."

My guts had officially migrated to Siberia.

Yeah, I know, I'm supposed to be the successful business guru with the All Star credentials. But it's one thing to be a part of an existing corporate structure with processes, rules, and regulations, and a very specific job function. It's another to be solely responsible for creating this structure. I was a kid dribbling a basketball on his neighborhood blacktop dreaming of building a stadium and packing the seats on a nightly basis.

The good news was I had the benefit of not having to start from zero. So maybe instead of that neighborhood kid, I was more like a player turned professional coach who had just gotten promoted to general manager. And I planned to be more Larry Bird than Isaiah Thomas!

To do this I was going to have to rely on my various start-up experiences over the past ten years, from that campus organization to the natural skin care company to the significant role I played in launching the Brazilian subsidiary of Schering-Plough. I had to trust that I had accumulated the necessary tools to get the job done. It was exhilarating and frightening at the same time, like the first time you took those training wheels off that bike and encountered your first hill.

But all that experience had one big drawback: I knew all the things that could go wrong. When you are a novice or doing something for the first time, your ignorance becomes a blanket shielding you from the worst of your failures. I had no such luxury. My eyes were wide open.

Still, my partners were counting on me to pull through. I decided to start with my five rules for starting a new company and take it from there. I also used a business plan template that had served me well in the past. With the steps clearly laid out before me, I strapped on my gear, put on the backpack, and told the pilot to take it up to 30,000 feet. Everything we know today as greatness began with a simple act of faith. Geronimo!

12: The 2nd Power Summit
January 29-31, 2010

So there we were, six weeks into our new venture and waist-deep in goals, plans, and tasks. There were several items on the near-term agenda that required in-person consultation (such as discussing financing and partnership agreements), so Omar arranged to fly out to California again at the end of January for our second Power Summit.

Our agenda was ambitious. Over the next 48 hours we charged ourselves with the following tasks:

- Build the Blog/Website
- Produce several weeks worth of blog content
- Finalize Business Plan
- Work out Division of Labor
- Agree on financing arrangement
- Brainstorm marketing strategies
- Lay the groundwork for total web domination
- Compile web resources; distribution lists
- Decide on names for our Imprints
- Launch the Blog

Little did we know that in addition to all that work, we'd also be dealing with mounting frustration, the first official TPC blow-up, and the beginning of burnout.

13: Do You Know the Way to San Jose?

Omar

Just one month into 2010, and two months since the birth of TPC, and I was as nervous as a pre-wedding groom. I'd made the commitment, but now I had to show up and do my best to keep this relationship progressing. Only problem was, my first marriage ended in divorce!

Still, I was determined to do whatever was needed to protect our union. One of the most obvious barriers was distance. Video chatting had helped us maintain visual contact over the past six weeks, but we'd all had our collective fingers crossed that I'd get the job I'd interviewed for at that Bay Area pharmaceutical company and soon be making the move to California. The hiring manager had indicated he wanted to bring me back for a final round of interviews at the end of January, but as the days turned into weeks, I'd still heard nothing. I was disappointed—I'd been focusing a little too much on the cosmic timing of this opportunity as a signal from the universe that this cross-country collaboration was meant to be.

Well, the universe works in mysterious ways. During the third week in January I learned that I would not be coming back for a second round of interviews. The company had decided to promote someone from within for the position. I was seriously bummed. But Stephanie and James reminded me that this was only a temporary setback and that TPC was still full speed ahead. In fact, we made plans to meet the following weekend.

The last week of January I got some more bad news. My 94-year-old grandmother had come down with a case of the shingles, which threw her immune system out of whack. She was in the ER in Pittsburgh and wasn't breathing on her own. These episodes had increased in frequency over the past year and a half, but this was by far the most serious. My priorities had been reordered on the spot. The first order of business was to buy my parents a last minute plane ticket to Pittsburgh so they could support my Aunt who was with Grandma at the hospital.

I texted Stephanie with the news and let her know our weekend retreat might be off. I decided to wait to buy my ticket to San Jose; if Grandma got worse, I'd be heading to Pittsburgh instead. Over the days that followed, I thought about how my grandmother had started her own successful hair salon in the fifties and how this business had sustained her when my grandfather passed in 1977. I realized that entrepreneurism was literally in my blood. So after a few touch-and-go days, by mid-week Grandma had improved enough to give me the confidence to proceed with booking my flight to the West Coast.

By Friday, I knew I'd made the right decision. Grandma was suffering from pneumonia but they'd removed the breathing tubes. My dad assured me they had everything under control. Boarding the plane in JFK, I turned my mind back to TPC, wondering how productive we would be with nearly 48 hours at our disposal. One thing was for sure, this would be a defining moment for the three of us.

14: Buh, Bye Honeymoon

Stephanie

To be honest, I didn't want to host the 2nd Power Summit in late January. James and I had planned to escape to Tahoe that weekend for some much needed R&R, away from TPC stuff, so when Omar offered to fly out, my first thought was "Damn!" But if I've learned anything about the grind towards greatness, it's that fun and relaxation always take a backseat to work. Well, nine times out of ten. And this was one of those times.

Emotionally and physically, I was starting to show signs of wear and tear. We'd set an ambitious timetable for our various goals, and we were working, literally, 'round the clock. Then, just when things started getting super-busy, my immune system called a time out. I came down with a pretty bad cold that took me out of commission for several days. Which in turn put me several days behind schedule on all the crap I had to do. I started to wonder if I would ever catch up.

I sent James to fetch Omar from the airport Friday night, and tried to do some meditating to get my head right. We had a lot of work to do, a lot of decisions to make. I needed to calm down and get grounded.

Omar's flight got in pretty late, so thankfully we didn't talk any business after the boys got back. Just caught up on friend stuff, and then called it a night. In the morning, I suggested we start the day by taking a hike through the forest. I've found that close proximity to the redwoods does wonders for clearing my head. The boys were all over it.

The hike was awesome. Not just for the fresh air and opportunity to stretch our legs, but because it gave James and Omar an opportunity to bond. You see, I am the link that connects James to Omar. James is my most significant other, and Omar is one of my most cherished Kindred, but the two of them had only hung out together twice prior to the First Power Summit and were still getting to know each other. I intentionally hung back during our walk so that the boys could get their bond on. It was actually quite heartwarming to watch, as two people I am incredibly close to developed their own closeness. The circle was complete.

But alas, the warm fuzzies could only last so long. After breakfast, we fired up our respective laptops and tackled our To-Do lists. Now don't get me wrong, we all work incredibly well together, and have a genuine fondness for one another, but three strong personalities can only co-exist for so long before some sort of power struggle erupts. It's simple relationship physics—one person who is always right + another person who is always right = a whole lot of yelling when you encounter a difference of opinion.

15: You're Not Supposed to Say That in a Power Summit!

James

"F*ck you!" Stephanie screamed at me. Damn. I was waiting for her head to twist around.

So much evil in that pretty little face! Ms. Nature Lover basically ripped me into confetti, all because we disagreed on a few words for my latest blog, "Working Together: Smart, Dumb or Just Plain Crazy?" The words that started it all? These:

My version: How the hell will we pull this off?
Her version: How the hell are we gonna pull this off?
See the difference?

She argued her point; I held true to mine. Our verbal jousting went back and forth, like Bruce Lee against Chuck Norris in the grand finale—until she almost murder-death-killed me with an explosive "You know what? F*ck you!" Then she got up and walked outta the house. Poof. Gone.

What a great start to our 2nd Power Summit, huh? Omar, seated next to me, was like, "Uh…well…oooookay."

Our heated disagreement had spilled over into a lover's quarrel. I take the blame for letting that happen. Bad move, James.

But we're passionate people, hell bent on safeguarding our craft like Spartan warriors. In this case, our craft was the written word. As any writer will tell you, we commit our souls to each word we download from our heads, so be careful with them. Writers are a ticking time bomb when it comes to the building blocks of our expressions. They're our babies, for real.

Stephanie had retreated from me, no doubt resisting the urge to introduce a skillet to my forehead. In her absence, Omar, the omnipotent salesman, reminded my stubborn butt of something I'd missed: Not only was Stephanie in charge of all blogs, she edited them, too. In other words, she knows edits and I was infringing on her area of expertise. That would be like Stephanie telling Omar how to construct a marketing plan—when Omar already has an MBA in Marketing.

We had defined our roles and I was invading her territory. It's a pride thing, I guess. But for our company's sake, we sometimes had to push pride aside. We couldn't get caught up in ego because if one person in our tripod acts all high-and-mighty over the other two, the pillars of The Pantheon Collective crumble.

Realizing this, I chilled. When Stephanie returned, Starbucks in hand, we talked it over, compromised, and smoothed things out. Kissed and made up like lovers, friends, and partners should do. And guess what? I eventually decided she was right.

That's our strength, the ability to swallow a little bit of pride and acknowledge another point-of-view. You can't shut out your compadres in a partnership; each of us has an opinion that must be voiced and heard, never ignored. This kind of compromise requires some negotiation and a whole lot of trust. That's how we do. We are Partners. We are Pillars. We are The Pantheon Collective. Word.

No more "f*ck you's"…for now.

16: Build It and They Will Come

Stephanie

So yeah, we hit a rough patch, lol. But it was a good experience to have early on, to learn that we were mature enough to disagree fiercely, vent freely, then kiss, make up, and move on.

So back to work we went.

The key component of our "launch" as a company was to build a website. Our blog/website was going to put us on the map, literally, so we wanted it to be an accurate representation of the TPC brand—functional, attractive, and full of useful information. A lot of thought and care went into designing our website.

There are a lot of expenses associated with starting a new business, and we tried to be very strategic about how we elected to spend our start-up funds. Fully embracing the DIY revolution and invoking the "Power of Three" whenever possible, we decided that rather than hire a web designer to build us a site, we would take a crack at doing it ourselves.

I served as webmistress for my previous two jobs, so I took the lead on the web stuff. Granted, it had been a minute since I'd had to build a website from scratch, but some things are just like riding a bike. After I got into the zone, all my HTML knowledge started coming back to me.

Not that this whole process wasn't without aggravation. First off, we had a helluva time trying to get the template we'd purchased (Thesis 1.6) to actually work. I spent many, many hours during the Power Summit troubleshooting technical issues. I was pulling my hair out and cursing up a storm at points (see previous chapter, lol). But I had to keep my eye on the prize—in 48 hours, we had a blog to launch.

The first set of decisions had to do with blog architecture. What was our desired color scheme? Main categories for the Nav bar? How would we organize the sections of our site? What information did we want to provide? What kinds of resources did we want to feature? Who should we include as "Friends of TPC"?

After we settled on the basic organization of our site, we moved on to discuss content. What was going to be our overall story arc? How many times a week would we blog? Who would be responsible for producing the original content?

All I can say is—it was a good thing Omar was physically here while we were building this thing. We had the benefit of being able to crowd around the computer to test out different layouts and fonts, tweaking this and changing that, until we got it just right. By the time we went to bed on Saturday night, we'd made some serious progress.

The finishing touch came to me in a dream. As my partners will tell you, we eat, sleep, and breathe TPC. Always thinking about ways to be tighter, better. The first thought in my head when I opened my eyes Sunday morning was—we need a picture of the Pantheon Kindred.

Since this was one of those rare occasions when the three of us were actually in the same zip code, we needed to find someone to take our photograph. But could I get ahold of a photographer on such short notice?

I called my photographer friend, Lisa Rose, who shot the cover image for *When Love Isn't Enough*. As luck (or fate) would have it, she was free to shoot some photos for us that afternoon. Serendipity strikes again!

The photo shoot went really well, and within hours Lisa had the proofs uploaded for us to review. There was something about seeing these pics that just made it all seem REAL. We were really doing this. The Pantheon Collective was official!

17: Blasting Off

We launched www.pantheoncollective.com on February 8, 2010 with our very first blogs. Simultaneously, we created a Facebook page and Twitter handle, and opened a Gmail account to receive company e-mail. Our objective was to leverage the blog and Facebook to attract and retain at least 1,000 followers/fans in the first year. After blasting off e-mails to our respective distribution lists, and inviting the world via Facebook, we sat back to see how much traffic we would generate.

We received 128 visits the day we launched the site and visitors stayed on the site for an average of 12 minutes and 48 seconds, which was not too shabby for a brand new website. We published 24 blogs in 28 days and people continued to show up to watch the drama unfold. Omar was obsessed with tracking the numbers while Stephanie busted her rump on the *Sellout* edits and James continued with his rewrites. By the end of the first month, the blog was receiving 62 visits per day (over 1,000 visits in three weeks) and we had accumulated 93 Facebook fans.

With that going well, the TPC3 turned their attention to designing and printing business cards, securing our company PO Box, and selecting the book cover for *Sellout*. Our cover designer, Marion Designs, had provided us with several cover designs to choose from, so we decided to hold a contest on our blog and Facebook page to involve our fans in the process. We received over 100 votes and went with the cover the "people" had selected.

We also made plans to attend ASPICOMM Media's Self-Publishing Symposium in Harlem, NY on March 5, 2010. The one-day event would give us the opportunity to network with industry opinion leaders like Selena James of Kensington Books; Troy Johnson, founder and head of AALBC; Carol M. Mackey, head of Black Expressions Book Club; Tee C. Royal, founder of RAWSISTAZ; and New York Times bestselling author Mary "Honey B" Morrison. This event was of high strategic importance for us, as we prepared to take our plan to the next level.

18: The 3rd Power Summit
March 4-6, 2010

James

I traded The Bay Area's lazy ambiance for the Big City of Dreams. New York. Where high-rise billboards bathe in big city lights. New York. Where a trillion cabs paint the streets yellow as they maneuver around pedestrians, who are either unaware of or unfazed by the headlights. New York. Just three years before Omar, Stephanie, and I had met here and first discussed the possibility of building a business together, so it was serendipitous—as Stephanie would say—that we returned here to make our formal debut as publishing industry players.

Stephanie and I arrived at JFK Saturday evening and Omar picked us up. We literally left the west coast at breakfast and arrived in NYC at dinner time. We had scheduled this extremely short but necessary trip to attend the Self-Publishing Symposium, but before we got down to business, we had a little fun on the agenda—a Saturday night on the town involving fine dining and a lot of alcoholic injections.

I was excited, not just because I was in Jay Z's backyard, but I would finally meet my former literary agent for the first time (I'll call her Diana). Diana, a well-known agent in the game for nearly thirty years, once represented my manuscript *A Hard Man is Good to Find*—long before I even thought of going the indie route. I found her name in the Acknowledgements section of a book in my genre, placed her on top of my Agents-to-Contact list, and sent a query letter. Within six months, I received an agent-client agreement. I was so freakin' happy I almost exploded out of my military boots (I was still in the Navy at the time). I, James W. Lewis, aspiring best-selling author, had hurdled a wall that 98 percent of potential authors don't: Signed with a legit major player in the publishing industry. You couldn't tell me nothin'!

Diana was my agent for a little over a year, and she busted her butt on my behalf. But, alas, even that kind of clout couldn't seal the deal. The book was "too much of this" or "too little of that." Sometimes, publishers don't want to take a chance on a newbie. Typical publisher rejection mumbo-jumbo. Oh, well, we tried, and although we didn't get what we wanted, her expertise and guidance helped put the spit-shine on *A Hard Man*, making it more of a marketable, saleable book. Yes, I was disappointed, but ya gotta keep it movin', right? I still had dreams to fulfill! Just had to figure out another way to reach them.

Though we eventually parted ways, I was excited to finally meet Diana and convey my thanks for her mentorship and support. We picked her up at eight, and the moment Diana revealed her ultra diva self, we loved her! Witty, funny, and no-nonsense all wrapped in a mini but powerful package. Definitely a to-the-bone New "Yawker."

The four of us headed to The Red Cat, a cozy spot with a laid-back vibe and five-star service. We talked about TPC and the publishing industry, but also got to know each other on a personal level. Stephanie and Diana bonded like long lost twin sisters, from their knowledge of astrological signs to their lust for Johnny Depp. We flooded our glasses with mojitos, wine, and scotch, partying it up in a New York hot spot—laughin', clappin', hand slappin', and bubbly glass tappin'.

But amid the party-over-here kinship, I will never forget something Diana said. While discussing the plight of my manuscript, I described the influence that one of my favorite authors had on my writing process, and how reading his work for the first time pushed me to step my game up. The words she offered next left me speechless: Diana said my writing skills were not only superior to most of the manuscripts she'd read, but she thought I wrote better than that particular author! I had to keep my tear ducts in check when I heard that.

To have someone in the industry say something so... so... shoot, I don't know how to describe it. Like I was Popeye in serious need of spinach for strength and in she comes with a truckload of it. Mentioned in the same breath as the elite... that's... wow. What else do I need to say? It felt effin' good.

A true writer must wear many hats, but the most important is the "writer" hat. A writer must invest in the nuts-and-bolts of writing, those tiny building blocks that become the blueprint of just about everything we create. Writers need to keep their pen-to-paper skills on point, and Diana made me feel I was doing that. She had given my writing skills the much appreciated affirmation I needed to take the stage with confidence.

By New York standards, we shut down kinda early so we could get a good night's sleep. We had a big day ahead, which would require us to don yet another hat—the networking hat. Business cards in hand, TPC would finally make its grand debut.

19: One Step at a Time

Omar

It was a Sunday morning, and TPC was imitating that early bird out to get the proverbial worm. On the drive to Harlem, we bumped Rick Ross' "Everyday I'm Hustlin,'" our mood focused, but playful. Yes, today was a very important occasion, our coming out party if you will, but we were loose. We had planned for this moment and now it was just a matter of executing our plan. We were looking good, all shiny and brand new, and the world would soon know TPC came to play.

The moment we stepped off the elevator on the 2nd floor of the Schaumberg Center, site of ASPICOMM Media's Self-Publishing Symposium, I was assaulted by doubts as to whether we were in the right place. Those thoughts were quickly obliterated by one welcoming smile from symposium host, Renee Daniel Flagler. As the room filled up with attendees I began to get the sense that we had just been welcomed into an exclusive club of red pill takers, all awake to the vast possibilities that came with being independently published.

With each person I encountered, from Kenny Blue with Journey Publishing to radio host Ricky Young to Ron Kavanaugh, head of online giant Mosaic Books, the sensation of belonging, of coming home, increased. Possibilities flooded my mind as the excellent program commenced. I had forgotten to bring pen and pad but was able to take copious notes via my iPhone (a device for red pill takers if there ever was one!).

Taking advantage of every available opportunity to network, I quickly realized another shining example of the "Power of Three"… TPC was everywhere and on the lips of everyone present. People were clearly intrigued by the idea of three writers from different coasts joining forces to independently publish four books in twelve months while blogging about the entire process.

The fatedness of arriving and being in the exact right place at the exact right time pervaded the air. We had crossed a very important threshold, from unknown entity to industry player. It felt destined. We were on the right path. With one step at a time and six strong legs to carry us forward, we were on our way to accomplishing all our goals and more!

20: Finding Community

Stephanie

My experience at the Self-Publishing Symposium was also an incredibly positive one. I am very big on the concept of community, and feel that people can make great strides towards achieving their goals through strategic partnership. This search for community motivates every connection I make, and is one of the main reasons I decided to partner with James and Omar to start our publishing company.

The Self-Publishing Symposium was inspiring, not only because I was able to network with established publishing professionals and authors, but because I got to see firsthand Black entrepreneurship in action. As a woman of color, I cannot describe how empowering it was to sit in a room with this group of Black business owners, MBA holders, and glass ceiling shatterers. Incredibly accomplished and successful individuals. Talk about a Power Summit!

The theme of the day resonated deep in my soul, the way it does when destiny comes calling. There is no reason for us to be at the mercy of big business, "the man," if you will. We shouldn't have to compromise, conform, or be exploited and undercompensated. We can (and should) take control of our products, our process, and our profits. Black-owned. Employing and collaborating with people of color. Producing products for a multicultural (and underserved) audience. These are concepts I could totally get behind.

A few things about this group that stood out for me was the way we were welcomed into the fold, the genuine interest in our work, and folks' generosity in terms of time and counsel. When you're trying to rise to the top, it is common to encounter "haters" along the way, people who hoard their expertise because they view you as competition and want the fame and fortune all to themselves. I am happy to report that there was no such haterism on display at this event. Everyone was sincerely trying to uplift, empower, and inspire each other. This is the essence of what I define to be community, and I was thrilled to be in such good company. Definitely feelin' the love.

I left the symposium not only energized, but with a host of mentors who can serve as models for TPC as we climb this mountain. And when we get a ways up, we plan to turn around and help those who have bravely followed in our footsteps. Cause that's how we do—lifting as we climb. Amen.

21: Validation

James

I really didn't know what to expect when TPC rolled up in the Schaumburg Center, but I knew one thing: We possessed new attitudes, no longer three starry-eyed wannabes staring up a mountain wondering when we would finally stand on top. The TPC3 were steadily navigating up that mountain, the peak within reach, and the Self-Publishing Symposium would be yet another platform to push us higher. Hell, TPC could stand for The Peak Climbers.

I walked in with my partners all "Men's Wearhoused" out, ready to get my socialite mingle on. Always cool to reconnect with old friends like Troy Johnson and Tonya Marie Evans and make new ones like Wahida Clark, JJ Smith, and Ricky Young. We had dispersed to our own private meet and greets, three separate individuals on opposite ends of the room. And yet, we were a virtual mainframe, reminding everyone that it didn't matter whose hand they shook or card they received: Whether Omar, James, or Stephanie, we were still The Pantheon Collective.

But confidence aside, we came for a reason—to learn from those who had walked the hard road before us. And boy, did they deliver.

TPC took mad notes, soaking in a wealth of information from industry juggernauts. But the more I listened to them, the more my pride swelled. The speakers and panelists hit on the key points that all independent publishers should master, like how to self-promote and take charge of your destiny. Lacking big publisher distribution didn't necessarily mean a disadvantage; it was possible to reach targeted markets better than the big boys. They also mentioned different ways to break out from the crowd. TPC had already designed a marketing plan based on that exact premise. It was reassuring to confirm that we were on the right track.

Take online presence, for example. We were already implementing many of the strategies they discussed. And not just one person, either. Oh, no, how about three? You see the power in that? If not, think of three fighter planes honed in on a target. Three times the might, three times the muscle—and one obliterated mofo.

Our particular target? To become a major force in the publishing industry. I believed we were on the right path, the TPC train barreling forward, building steam to reach that dream. As I stared at the panelists, I fell into a daydream, watching an episode of our lives that I couldn't wait to see materialize: The three of us, all on stage, doing our own "paneling," passing a microphone back and forth. As we faced the audience, we dropped knowledge and answered a ton of questions.

Awww, I could see it all. The Pantheon Collective, industry experts and future panelists. Add that to the TPC gift bag along with the other ideas itching to become tangible.

22: I Need a Vacation

Stephanie

At the 3rd Power Summit, we outlined the phases of *Sellout* pre-production, and the associated deadlines for each phase. In order to have copies printed in time for our appearance at the BWRC in June 2010, we had to pick up the pace. I needed to finish my content edit, ASAP.

I was given a deadline of Sunday, March 14, 2010 for completing my edits, and to hit that mark, I pretty much had to embrace *Sellout* tunnel vision. What that means is, in every spare moment, I had to be reading. On the bus. In the waiting room at the doctor's office. Until 2:00 a.m. pretty much every night. All other areas of my life faded away as I hunkered down for this last push. Family gathering in San Ramon? Sorry fam, I'm working. Dinner with a girlfriend? Sorry hon, I'm working. Set the DVR to record Grey's Anatomy, 'cause, yup, you guessed it, I'm working.

Now mind you, I'd been experiencing fatigue and burnout for weeks. I mean, even the most mild-tempered, peace-loving individual is going to get cranky when they realize they are spending virtually every waking moment, on average six hours a day (in addition to my day job), hustlin'. I knew this venture was going to require dedication and commitment when I signed on, but to be honest, the reality of it was wearing on me. Especially when things I deemed more important (like spending time with my newborn nephew) got pushed aside. I was starting to wonder if the stress and strain was worth it. I mean, isn't this supposed to be fun and rewarding? My partners seemed to be having fun, but me, saddled with the most time-consuming of all the start-up tasks… Not so much.

But at the end of the day, I'm a trooper. I finished the *Sellout* edits around 5:00 p.m. on the 14th, which left me with six hours to eat, attend a virtual Power Summit, and complete the final homework assignment for my editing course (which I also got done, with seven minutes to spare). Yes, it felt great to have met a major deadline; I might have partaken in some sort of celebratory ritual if I hadn't been so exhausted.

Next on the To-Do list? Take Care of Me. As much as I hate to admit it, I'm not Superwoman, and if I was to be of any use to my partners, I had to carve out some time for the three Rs (Rest, Relaxation, & Rejuvenation) to address this burnout issue. I needed a solid three-day span (at least!) of not thinking about anything related to TPC in order to find my joy again and re-engage with the excitement of what it means to be embarking on this entrepreneurial enterprise with my two favorite guys. And I could definitely use a freaking massage. Was there money in the budget for a spa retreat?

FROM AUTHORS TO ENTREPRENEURS

23: Shoot, I Need a Vacation, Too!

James

Stephanie wasn't the only one out of gas. My tank was nearly on "E," too. Damn near running on fumes and I needed a fill up on Premium.

Stephanie had done her job on *Sellout*; now, it was my turn. But I wore other hats, too. At the time I was a full-time college student studying Kinesiology. I also worked at a veteran's assistance center, volunteered at a stroke center, and "daylighted" as a personal trainer at a local university. That may seem like a lot, but it all coincided with my intended career track in health and fitness.

I'm also one of those go-getters, pouncing on every opportunity, sometimes over-committing myself. But I honor my obligations and follow through with all of them. Blame it on the military upbringing. We don't stop until we complete the mission.

That meant I was always on the fly, flames under my shoes, as I skyrocketed out the door to my next "duty station." Unfortunately, I also had a manuscript to revise, so I had to get it in when I could fit it in. That usually entailed me burning the midnight oil, first doing homework, then manuscript rewrites. Stephanie had done such a great job that I agreed with most of her edits. But checking word-by-word, line-by-line takes time, and I was under the gun, my deadline for completing revisions set for March 22, 2010.

Stephanie and I had a nice system in place. As she finished edits on several chapters, she'd send them to me for rewrites. We were always working on the manuscript at the same time, with me a couple of chapters behind. When she finished, I was on Chapter 25 and only had five more to go.

24: Patience is a Virtue

Omar

I consider myself a pretty patient person. I also would say I'm generally positive and upbeat about most aspects of my life, especially TPC. But every now and then, frustration rears its penetrating proboscis and tries its best to poke into my skull and drain my positive mainframe. Now, I don't practice yoga, work out regularly enough, or have any great positive stress relievers, but I do have a philosophy that tends to work in frustrating situations such as the one I found myself in on Thursday, March 18, 2010.

TPC had been very successful thus far due to our maniacal focus on everything we could control and earnest attempts to influence the things we didn't control. This is not an original philosophy; Stephen Covey discussed these spheres in his landmark book *The Seven Habits of Highly Effective People*.

The first habit he discusses is Proactivity. Allow me to elaborate: In life, business, personal relationships, etc., there is this push/pull dynamic between those things we control and the things we don't. How much you are pushed or pulled by the gravity of these spheres is very much in your control.

The Sphere of Control is always smaller than the Sphere of Concern because there are fewer things within your control than things that can possibly concern you. The proactive approach means focusing 90 percent of your energy on the areas of your life you control and adjusting your attitude as it relates to those aspects in your life beyond your control. You can complain about the rain or you can get an umbrella, rain slicker, knee high boots, and keep it moving!

One of the more frustrating aspects of small business is the need to depend on third parties for goods and services to hit our deadlines as we rapidly approached the launch of *Sellout*. Stephanie experienced this dealing with our website provider; James with our book cover and author website designer; and I was up to my neck in it with the legal services company I hired to "officialize" our enterprise.

I paid $115 extra to expedite our paperwork so we would have it in 7-10 business days like their site promises, and I expected this deliverable to be met. Without a legal corporate entity, we couldn't purchase the ISBNs necessary to sell our books. Imagine my chagrin when day 11, 15, and 20 arrived post-purchase and still no documents. My frustration and stress levels were in the red line. Then I realized my error.

I had failed in my Sphere of Control by not following up with the company until day 20. I allowed the issue to snowball due to my inactivity. After taking control of the situation and making a few phone calls, I was assured that our packet would be in the mail within 24 hours. I was also able to get a full refund of the expedited fee, which is a testament to the company's professionalism. But an important lesson was learned. From here on out, I am adding a new proverb to my cadre of personal mantras: Patience is a virtue, but Proactivity is divine!

25: The 4th Power Summit
April 3-4, 2010

TPC was a long-distance relationship, with one partner in New Jersey and the other two pillars in California. We conducted about 85 percent of our business remotely. But at the start of our "adventure," we made the firm commitment that every six weeks we would get together for an in-person Power Summit. The creativity that flowed when the three of us sat in a room together was truly magical, and we were committed to hosting Power Summits as often as we could manage.

We convened in early April for the 4th Power Summit, and as usual had a packed agenda. As we barreled toward the launch of *Sellout*, our To-Do list was growing faster than we could cross things off. But we were one determined set of Kindred, and after our ritual hike through the forest, we rolled up our sleeves and got to work. Some of the items on our agenda:

- Group discussion of final *Sellout* revisions
- First quarter budget review
- Draft marketing plan for *Sellout*
- Draft Author agreements

- Finalize TPC logo
- Film videos for TPC TV
- Create April Task List
- Sign LLC papers (and celebrate!)

Not only did we achieve off-the-chain productivity, but we also did some celebrating as well. Work hard, play hard—it's the TPC way!

26: Doing What I Do

Omar

Did I ever tell you why I love flying so much? Flying is the perfect allegory for how I live my life. Check it. From the moment the plane takes off until it lands safely at the designated destination, I have ceded control over my own safety. The only control I retain is how I use my time (do I sleep the trip away, or apply my time in a more productive manner?) and my attitude toward turbulence (does every jolt signify impending doom, or will it smooth out as it almost always does?).

Flying reminds me to enjoy the ride, use my time wisely, and not allow a few bumps to ruin my short trip. When I fly, I let go completely. Such a freeing feeling!

On the flight from JFK to San Jose (a flight I made with less than two minutes to spare, btw), I had two primary goals: finish reading *Sellout* and draft the basic skeleton of the *Sellout* marketing plan. Reading and marketing—two of my favorite passions! The six hours zipped by.

Stephanie picked me up at the airport and I promptly began downloading my thoughts on *Sellout*. The book was damn good, but some character tweaks were needed to take it from a good book to a *great* book. As we got closer to Santa Cruz, I hoped I would be able to convince James to go back in and rewrite certain passages. This was crucial, because ideas of how to market his masterful work were flooding my brain. *Sellout* would have four main target audiences: Black women who had never dated interracially, black woman who had, white women who had never dated interracially, and white women who had. The book would have to be positioned differently for each of the distinct audiences, but if we did it right, I was sure that *Sellout* could be a massive hit. I couldn't wait to drop all this on James, and kept my fingers crossed that he would go along with my suggestions.

Now that I had confirmed the quality of the product, I needed everything to line up. It was marketing plan time. Time to do what I do!

27: TPC is LLC!

James

Oh, sh**! It's official: TPC is an LLC. That's what we be.

If I had any leftover doubt regarding how far Omar, Stephanie and I had gotten in this business venture, the thick burgundy notebook that arrived in the mail with "The Pantheon Collective (TPC) LLC" on the spine squashed it all. The dictionary defines **real** as "being an actual thing; having objective existence; not imaginary." The Pantheon

Collective was *real* now. On March 23, 2010, TPC became a Limited Liability Corporation.

When I first opened the box, it was like unwrapping a Christmas present already knowing what's inside—yet still feeling all giddy about it. Yeah, we'd covered major ground the last three months to establish TPC, so you can say we'd been legit for a while. But for business owners, you can't *really* call yourself legit until your business has a nationally recognized stamp of approval. As an LLC, those three letters legally, professionally, financially—and any other appropriate "ly" word you can think of—established TPC as a *com-pa-ny*. Hell, a freakin' corporation. Set us apart from "hobbyist" and made what we're doing official. Sort of like a lawyer who earns the letters ESQ or a doctor with an MD.

It's crazy to think what only lived in our heads as a fantasy had become an actual entity. Something tangible, an enterprise. We had joined the ranks of dreamers and visionaries who'd succeeded in transforming a figment of their imagination into something you can see, taste, and feel. We were slowly achieving the great American dream—from caterpillars to butterflies. Felt pretty good, you know?

But guess what? If we were going to call ourselves an LLC, we had to act like an LLC. Simply put, don't talk about it, be about it. That meant documenting our minutes; maintaining company ledgers; tracking income and expenses; upholding the operating agreement; filing and paying business taxes; augmenting capital for overhead; separating personal assets from business assets; managing duties of individual

TPC members; acquiring additional liability protection... damn! The learning curve was no joke, and though we used the "Power of Three" to optimize our business and avoid common start-up mistakes, this was a lot of freakin' information. And we still had to debut this little novel called *Sellout*, our first tangible product.

Did I say, oh sh**, already?

28: We Are Family

Stephanie

While there was plenty of business to conduct at the 4th Power Summit (such as drafting the *Sellout* marketing plan and fleshing out the *Sellout* revisions), there was also a lot to celebrate. This was the first time the TPC Kindred had seen each other since receiving the LLC papers, so not only was this the moment where we officially SIGNED the papers to officialize the partnership, this was also our opportunity to celebrate!!!

We'd come a loooong way since our decision last December 2009 to join forces and start this publishing venture. We'd had our share of ups and downs, stresses and strains, joys and triumphs. But putting pen to paper to legally bind ourselves to one another, and to our baby (aka TPC) was a whole other level of commitment and achievement. I'd always dreamed about owning my own business, but I never imagined how fast that dream would materialize once

I set my mind to turning dreams to reality. The unimaginable had become tangible. TPC was LLC!

The official signing took place at my brother's house on Easter Sunday, which was very meaningful to me, personally. Not only were my nearest and dearest on hand to celebrate (and document!) the moment for us, but the family atmosphere really mirrored what this moment signified for us. James, Omar, and myself had taken a step that moved us beyond friends. We were now three individuals with a vested interest in maintaining this long-term relationship. Bound and bonded, for better or worse. Partners, Parents, and Spouses. We were FAMILY.

So as me and my two husbands moved forward into the great unknown, I knew we would always look back on this moment with great pride and accomplishment. The moment when our respective paths crossed, converged, and set off in a new direction. The moment we went from Authors to Publishers, taking control of our destinies. I couldn't wait to see what came next!

29: Revision Hell

James

Any writer will tell you writing is about *re*writing. You never get it right the first time. That pretty much applies to the work of all artists. You think George Lucas wrapped up *Star Wars* after only one take for each scene? Hell naw.

Action. Cut. Action. Cut. Scene after scene, take after take, over and over again. Change this, change that. R2D2, wobble this way; C3PO, stand that way; Luke jump here; Han Solo run there; Princess Leia, touch up those two cinnamon roll hairpieces.

And then finally, *Star Wars* is done! Perfect!

But hold on: Once Georgey compiled all the movie footage, you think he kept everything? I say again, hell naw. The grim reapers of cinematography—aka the editing team—sliced and diced scenes on the chopping block, many never to be viewed by the public. Everybody involved with the film left their blood, sweat, and tears in each scene—only for a few know-it-alls with a little power to say, "We don't like that scene. Cut it."

Jacked up, huh? Who did those mofos think they were, dissecting the artist's masterpiece?

Well…we all know how *Stars Wars* did at the box office. It's considered one of the greatest movies of all time. Anyone involved with shaving off its cinematic "baby fat" must've known something.

That's similar to what I went through with *Sellout*. This book is my baby, and I'm the proud father. Or maybe "fauthor?" Whatever, the point is, after two professional edits (where I'd already made cuts and changes based on editor comments), I was still rewriting. Why? Because it's the TPC way.

We critiqued each other's work. Stephanie and Omar had become my new TPC editorial team, and they poked, prodded, and plucked away at parts of my manuscript like a frog in a science lab. Deconstructed my characters to the bone, unearthing the how's and why's of their psyches. They were more like book character psychiatrists than partners, providing substantive feedback.

Which meant...more revisions. All while competing against the clock. Got a deadline and my time was almost up. But it's all good. The owners of TPC are voracious readers, and I respected my partners' opinions. Some of their comments stung, but I agreed with most of them, mainly because Stephanie and Omar could back up why the character should do this or do that. They knew my characters almost better than I did. So I had no problem rewriting, especially since I believed the changes would make the story better. Going back to the drawing board sucks sometimes, but artists understand it's necessary to produce a quality product.

Besides, their books came next and it was *my* turn to slice and dice.

30: New J.O.B. Less T.I.M.E. for TPC

Omar

I consider time to be my most valued asset. Time is finite and fickle. You never know how much you've got left so it behooves you to maximize it.

I've always been a master multi-tasker. Compared to President Obama I probably look like a slacker, but I do pretty well for myself. Multi-tasking is a lot like those guys and gals you've seen spinning 20 plates at a time atop tall, thin rods or sticks. But what happens when all those plates come crashing down at once?

In January 2010 I was spinning a job I was soon to leave, rewrites on my debut novel, and TPC. In February I dropped the job, added a girlfriend, started a ten-week novel writing class, and threw in a few random spoken word performances, including my first feature at a Black History Month event at Manhattanville College. Man, those days were great: spending plenty of QT with my lady, going to bed late and waking up even later, working out, midday happy hours, and time to spare for taking care of TPC business.

By April I'd started a new job in a new industry. I was joining an interactive events company called UNISON that used proprietary technology to connect participants in live meetings and give audiences more power than the presenter. I was super excited about the opportunity to come into a company with a great concept, and help take it to the next level. But my life had to change. Overnight. Soon I was waking up at 6:30 a.m. to try to work out, then driving 49 miles to Nyack, NY, busting my ass at the office until 7:00 p.m. or so, and driving back home. The novel writing class was thankfully off my plate, but I had more work than ever to do to get *One Blood* in shape for publication in 2011. Quality time with my honey had been cut in half (not acceptable), and TPC business was really starting to heat up as we moved into the pre-print and pre-marketing phase.

We were launching and maintaining TPC TV, TPC Flickr, Facebook, and Twitter. We were also talking to lawyers, tax advisors, PR professionals, logo designers, and promotional giveaway vendors, to name a few. Not to mention registering for book expos and conferences to get ready for *Sellout* in June...WHEW!

I realized that I had so many things to master, but I needed to first master myself and my use of time before I could effectively serve any of them. I was only one man with 24 hours to give to the world. Then an idea occurred to me... what if I gave up sleep?

31: Website Issues

James

An author's website is an important component for building a brand. It's the author's "flagship," if you will, where a visitor can hop onboard, take a short trip, and learn all about that author's journey—which is why websites are still vital for flaming a buzz and hooking new readers, even in the new age of social media. Many authors find readers simply by posting blogs on their website. Yes, social media has become an important tool in the author's ever-growing kit, but not everyone does Facebook or Twitter, so how else can they find you? A website.

A busted website will tell you a lot about an author, too. My first website was just that—busted. Like low-budget busted. Straight-to-video, C-movie busted. If websites had a Razzie awards equivalent, I would've won.

When I first bought my domain name and hosting services back in 2003, I felt like a man on a mission! My own website with my name—jameswlewis.com—was about to join the other billion "stars" in cyberspace. Nice! That meant someone from Japan would know James W. Lewis…if they could find me. No sweat. All I needed were the pages to go with it (About Me, Links, Gallery page, yada-yada).

"I'll just build it myself," I had said.

And I did. I bought Microsoft Frontpage and went to work, using the software's templates. That was my first mistake. The templates were kindergarten-ish, but I didn't care. I was building my own website!

I thought I was making big things happen! Thinking myself a web design genius—who'd never designed any site at all—I had this crazy psychedelic color scheme, something like grey, yellow, and green all around. Straight out of a 60's comic book. Uneven borders, zigzaggy fonts, no worthwhile content. And to top off my masterpiece, I used a black-and-white 12-year-old sailor pic for my homepage. Kinda corny, but it sounded like a good idea back then.

I was so proud of myself! I let all my writer friends know about my tight new site. Yup, had my own Guestbook and everything. Well, word eventually got to my literary agent and she set me straight *big* time. She reminded me that not only did my ugly-ass website represent me as an up-and-coming author, I was representing her, too. And what I'd created was DOA.

So I went back at it, studying other author websites for guidance and ideas. I spent an entire weekend overhauling www.jameswlewis.com. Found a better template and got a professional headshot for the homepage. Eventually, I landed on a style that I'm still using today.

As we got closer to my book launch, I realized I needed to step my web game up even more. Technology changes constantly, and you need to update your website's look often to keep it fresh. Not that I needed fancy flash movies or anything like that, but nothing entirely bare-bones bland, either. The current site is ten times better than that first piece of crappola. Thank you, Wordpress!

32: When Planning Meets Reality

Omar

One of my favorite phrases of all time is "man plans and the universe laughs"—a not so subtle wink at how little control we have in our lives. Still, as Winston Churchill once famously said, "He who fails to plan is planning to fail." Here at TPC, we have grand plans, masterful plans, "insert superlative here" plans!

For example, we plan to shake up the publishing world with our innovative business approach, collective talent, and unwavering support from our fans. We plan to sell thousands of books and hit the Bestsellers lists. And we plan to succeed at all we do, blazing a trail for those who follow.

Our ambition knows no bounds.

When we set off on this independent publishing journey, we knew it was going to be a lot of work, and naively thought we had most of our bases covered. But we aren't psychics, and it is impossible to predict every curve and bend on the winding path to greatness.

One thing we planned very deliberately were specific financial investments designed to establish ourselves as a legitimate business, build our web presence, conduct photo shoots and the like, attend conferences, and purchase the products and services necessary to publish *Sellout* and future TPC books. But we started to see cracks in our blueprint as the expenses started piling up.

We quickly realized that for all our careful planning, we had grossly underestimated our start-up costs, outlays we had to make before we even printed and sold our first book. Like a newlywed couple building their dream house from the ground up, we had sunk a lot of cash into the money pit and still had no roof over our heads.

Still, it's all good. The great thing about plans is that like leaves in the fall, they are designed to change. As small business owners, we knew the key to success was to remain flexible while employing outside the box thinking to find creative solutions to our problems. Thankfully, this is one of our greatest assets. And besides, with the launch of *Sellout* just six weeks away, we were in way too deep to turn back!

33: The Cost of Doing Business

Stephanie

One of TPC's greatest challenges was figuring out how to stretch our initial investment to cover the wide variety of start-up costs associated with launching a new business. When we had our initial funding discussion at the 1st Power Summit, we each agreed to contribute $5000 as seed funding for TPC. At the time, $15,000 seemed like more than enough to start our company and launch *Sellout*. After all, with the various skills we were bringing to the table, coupled with our energy, enthusiasm, and Do-It-Yourself mentality, we assumed we could get most of the work done ourselves.

Then the realities of time and burnout set in, and we decided to outsource certain tasks. After hiring folks to design the TPC logo and the *Sellout* book cover, as well as preparing our LLC formation documents and putting an attorney on retainer, we'd already spent about $7,000 and had yet to print ONE book. And as quotes came in from publicists and accountants, not to mention the marketing and promotions for the *Sellout* launch, we were all sitting around scratching our heads, turning over rocks to see where we might be able to find another couple grand.

I admit, I experienced sticker shock *several* times when I got quotes back from folks. I wasn't born with deep pockets, and work in education (i.e. not a member of the six-figure club), so the thought of dropping several thousand dollars on *one* product or service seemed insane to me. But folks always say, "You've got to spend money to make money." TPC was trying to build a serious enterprise here, an empire if you will, and we were not willing to cut corners on quality. If we had to drop mad cash to get a logo designed, so be it.

So as we burned through our initial investment, we scrutinized every possible expense, evaluating what was essential, and what could be put off. We had to determine what tasks could be handled in-house, and when we needed to employ a "professional." And we had to prioritize.

Did we really need to hire someone to do our bookkeeping, or could we get by in the interim with Quicken or Quickbooks? Did we really need to hire someone to design James' website, or could we build it ourselves like we did with the TPC website? Every time we met, we had to make decisions like these, taking into account timelines, deadlines, and our own personal limitations.

After all, as much as we may "think" we're publishing superheroes, at the end of the day we're just three passionate and ambitious humans with day jobs, mortgages, bills, families, and significant others that were all competing for our time and limited resources. But TPC was determined to push on and keep hustling, because when we finally reach that point where we're holding our published books in our hands, we knew it would all be worth it...

34: The Cost of Doing Business, Part 2

Stephanie

In May 2010, the TPC blog went dark for about a week due to a mandated rest, recovery, and time-out period brought on by a major TPC blowout. The TPC3 had fought before, as is normal and natural in even the strongest relationships, but the blow-up that occurred mid-May was of such a serious magnitude that I wondered if we would be able to come out on the other side intact…

James wrote early on regarding his reservations about going into business with friends. I never took his concerns very seriously, living in a happy, delusional state about the sheer indestructibility of the TPC3—until the blow-up. Until I got to a point where I could barely stand the sight of these two men, much less imagine being in business with them for the foreseeable future. I can honestly say that in four years of dating (with James) and kindredship (with Omar), I had never been so angry. I was ready to walk away from it all. I was that mad.

As with most arguments, it all started with a miscommunication. But it quickly snowballed into an issue that had me thinking twice about whether or not it had been the best idea to go into business with a friend and boyfriend. When you reach an impasse in a regular professional context, the disgruntled party is either fired or quits. But as

I contemplated submitting my letter of resignation to TPC, it became clear that there was no way for me to exit this business partnership without doing irreparable damage to the personal relationships the partnership was built upon.

That was when I started my meditation about the other "costs of doing business." The human costs, the interpersonal costs. How a business disagreement could threaten friendships and inflict very real damage to people. James and I actually had to sit down at the end of this and make a pact that we would never let TPC break us up. If you had asked me in the beginning if an explicitly-stated agreement like that was necessary, I would have scoffed. But live and learn, I guess. There is a reason folks caution not to mix business with pleasure.

I'm relieved to report that TPC made it through the storm. We're healing and moving forward, committed to this (ad) venture we've undertaken. As Booker T. Washington once said, "Success is to be measured not so much by the position that one has reached in life… as by the obstacles which he has overcome while trying to succeed." With that in mind, TPC is definitely on track to achieve some extraordinary success. Onward and upward…

35: Too Many Damn Hats!

James

I usually sport a skin-fade, but even if I rocked dreadlocks I probably would've yanked half those bad boys out, just like the weeds in my backyard. I mean, damn, what the hell did we get ourselves into with this whole_publisher-small business-author thing? *And* all at the same time to boot! *And* while fighting the clock for a book launch in less than six weeks!

F*#k!

I was supposed to have been kickin' back, watchin' ball on TNT while sippin' on a brew, yet was *I*? Hell no. Like all hustlers on a steady grind, I was wearing too many damn hats—and I still had more I'd yet to slap on this big ol' forehead of mine (like selling my book).

It's not like I was a stranger to the madness. When I was active duty in the Navy, I also wore many hats—supervisor, counselor, manager, and sailor, among other things. When I retired in 2009, I chopped that list down to college student and community volunteer. I was pretty content wearing only two hats… until TPC came along. Then the schizophrenia really exploded: I added business owner, blogger, researcher, promoter, "Facebooker"… damn. I even added "Twitterer" to the mix. At first, I didn't think I'd give a "twit," but now I be twitting (or is it, "tweeting?"), too.

As a result, I woke up in the AM, then went to bed in the AM. Every hour awake was an opportunity to push forward on something. Can't waste time. Got too much to do. *Way* too much. I had a grade-point-average to keep up. Two partners depending on me. A book to get ready. A blog to write. Conferences. Research. Copyedits. Power Summits. Homework.

Hold up. Let me scream right quick ... okay, I feel a little better.

I'd signed on for this, though. I'd always wanted to wear the hat "business owner." Now, I do. Yeah, it was a headache at times, but I'd rather have a headache from working hard on TPC and everything else than be bored out of my mind because I don't have anything going on. I'm just glad I have two other pilots (and one who is my personal co-pilot) to fly this fighter jet with me because, damn, let me tell you, trying to manage all this sh*t ain't no joke.

But, don't get it twisted—I'm still lovin' this. Let's just hope I can keep these hats from falling off.

36: Sellout *Edits are Done!*

Stephanie

Mission Accomplished! I am happy to report that around 4:00 p.m. on May 23, 2010, I finished the FINAL *Sellout* copyedit. Woo Hoo! My primary contribution to the pre-production of TPC's debut novel was in the bag, off my plate, signed, sealed, and delivered. I was ready to throw a huge party up in here to celebrate.

This whole entrepreneurial experiment was proving to be quite the see-saw... Up, down. Up, down. TPC had just come through the requisite low, but thankfully, I found myself on the way back up, basking in the pride and accomplishment of a job well done. Special shout-out to my brother Bill for being a one-man cheering section, my girls for talking me down off the ledge as I toyed with filing for divorce from my two husbands (lol), and J-Dub, for loving me through the hard times and appreciating all the sacrifices I've made to keep this train moving forward. I couldn't have made it through this hell-ish month without y'all.

I was looking forward to wearing a different "hat" for a few months. Next up on my plate was coordinating the printing and distribution of *Sellout*, getting all our business ducks in order (bookkeeping system, budget audit and projections, acquainting myself with the Small Business Administration), and building a couple more websites (a revamp of www.stephaniecasher.com and redesign of www.jameswlewis.com). Then I got to turn my attention to the pre-production of my novel, *When Love Isn't Enough*, which was way exciting. But what I was most excited about was I get to put my writing hat back on, for the first time in too long, and work on the revision of *Soul Mates* (the sequel to *When Love Isn't Enough*).

Of all the things I'd given up to become a business owner, my writing time was the most unexpected casualty. Hopefully I still had the ability to conjure my creative juices at will.

But before all that, I was taking a deep breath and scheduling some downtime. As we barreled towards the launch of *Sellout*, the pressure shifted to Omar (marketing) and James (promotion). I'd set the productivity bar pretty dang high—hoping they could keep up!

37: Showtime!

Omar

Alright! It's the 4th quarter with six seconds on the clock. James broke ankles with a vicious crossover rewrite on *Sellout* and tied the game with the Power of Three from the corner. Stephanie blocked the independent publishing haterz with a tremendous copyedit that gave us the ball back with little time to score. And those of you who have downloaded the TPC Business Plan and Marketing Plan know that I get Jordan-esque when it comes to late-game heroics.

When it comes to marketing and promotion in these exciting digital times, you have to pick and choose your spots carefully. It's a simple formula: craft the right product, get it in front of the right audience, and give them the right incentive to pick it up. I had been visualizing this moment for years. Way before I ever knew I would be teaming up with Stephanie and James.

I knew that all the writer's conferences I'd attended over the years, all the research I'd done, all the books on the business of publishing I'd read, all the on-the-job training I got from my career as a marketing executive in the pharmaceutical industry, and all I'd invested in honing my craft would someday come down to one shot. Just. Like. This.

When it comes to launching a product—any product— you really only get one shot to get it right. I'd been waiting for this moment since I first texted Stephanie nearly seven months ago. And now that Stephanie has given me the ball, it was as good as game over. Whether it's writing top-tier, top-notch books, superbly editing said books, or marketing and promoting, TPC doesn't miss!

38: Almost There

James

Approximately 5,172,525. That's the number of edits I made to *Sellout*.

All right, I'm exaggerating. But I stared at the manuscript so many times, excerpts of the book were probably branded into the whites of my eyeballs. Rewrite after rewrite after f*ckin' rewrite. Up all hours of the day *and* night, trying to beat the clock, deadline approaching—sheesh!

But the manuscript *finally* made it to the typesetter's hands for interior design. Next step was to upload for printing, where we would receive a proof copy. We were in the fourth quarter, baby, approaching two minutes on the clock.

Still, I was *wor-ried*. I won't lie—anxiety whipped my ass.

Why? Because I was second guessing myself, asking questions like: Did I catch all the errors? Is *Sellout* a good story? Will people like it? Are we going to make the deadline? What if something goes wrong? Is it...

I felt a ton of pressure weighing down on me. I was finishing up a tough school semester, which took a huge load off my back, but I still had a battleground going on in my head, consisting of doubt, fear, and all those topsy-turvy emotions that cause you to throw in the towel.

But that's when people rise to the occasion, right? Well, I definitely had to do that. I was not only The Pantheon Collective's debut author, but I was debuting *me*, James W. Lewis, to the public. That meant I had to look right, talk right, act right, smell right, walk right, sit right, stand right—all that sh*t. I didn't have just bricks on my shoulders; I felt like the damn Great Wall of China was taking a piggy-back ride on me.

But that's natural, right? Every author experiences these mental humps, especially before their first book comes out. I'm no different. My dream was materializing before my eyes, so I also felt joy, pride, a sense of accomplishment—all those emotions that made me say, "I'm not throwing in no towel! Hell naw!"

And with the proof copy in hand, it was real. No turning back.

I'll tell you what, though, creating a top-notch story in written format is extremely difficult—plot, character development, pace, lively dialogue—and *Sellout* needed all these ingredients mixed in to create the "hot" book. But even though I'd given it my all, I knew some readers wouldn't like the taste of *Sellout*. Can you imagine anyone calling your newborn an ugly-ass baby?

Of course, I expected people to love my book, too. I'd hoped for five-star reviews that would start a buzz. Truth was, I really didn't know what to expect in terms of reader response. Nobody can predict that.

Luckily, my two partners became my consultants, confidantes, book doctors, and cheering section. We had created our own two-man, one-woman—and you know the word is coming—pantheon. Who would've thought the seed we planted three years would blossom into a sturdy tree bearing fruit?

Through brainstorming a company name, tagline, and mission statement; designing a book cover and company logos; attending dozens of webcam Power Summits; writing blogs; creating a website; manuscript editing and rewrites; making business decisions; arguing on email, in-person, text, *and* on the phone; typesetting the book's interior; and traveling cross-country…whew!

We did a lot in six months. I applaud my partners for convincing me to ride this crazy roller coaster, and the way I see it, we're still at the beginning of this loopity-loop.

39: Proof is in the Mail

Stephanie

In this business, as in life, situations fall into one of two categories—things you can control, and things you can't control. I could control my own level of productivity, and whether or not I met my personal deadlines, but once I passed the ball off to a partner or collaborator, I had to accept that things were now dependent on the work ethic and efficiency of someone else. Someone who may or may not feel the sense of urgency I did regarding deadlines and timelines. Having the ball in someone else's hands was stressful, especially during this particular phase of *Sellout* pre-production. We had cut things so close that the slightest delay at this point could result in not having books printed in time for the Black Writer's Reunion and Conference.

So even though finishing the *Sellout* copyedit was a huge weight off my shoulders, I still wasn't able to relax. Not until all the pre-production tasks had been completed. Thankfully, this time around, we'd picked the most amazing partners to collaborate with. We enlisted the help of Jessica Tilles at TWA Solutions to do the *Sellout* typesetting, and not only did she do a fantastic job, she turned it around in record time (despite the multitude of changes we sent her way in the 11th hour.)

On June 7, 2010, we had the final files for *Sellout* ready to upload for printing. After we completed the upload, we crossed our fingers that our printer/distributor, Lightning Source, would be just as quick and efficient.

Lightning Source gets high grades from me in terms of speed and customer service. The upload process was fairly straightforward, and you can log into your account any time to check the status of your order. I was VERY pleased to receive an email just three days later notifying us that the *Sellout* proof had been generated, and was on its way. James would be holding his book in his hands by the weekend! Of course we weren't done yet; we still had to proof the proof (lol), but the anticipation of receiving the tangible product of months and years worth of labor was SO exciting.

The release of TPC's debut novel was imminent!

40: Fifth Times the Charm

Omar

One of my biggest flaws is that I don't really take the time to reflect on key accomplishments in my life. Take birthdays, for example. I stood on the precipice of my 33rd year on this earth and it was just funny to me how I'd gone from not being able to imagine myself at age 30 (back when I was 21) to having so many ambitions that I needed every 365 days I could get!

Don't get me wrong, I always celebrate success. But I move on from those moments so fast it's almost as if they never happened. This may be because I always expect to be successful no matter the endeavor, and I wind up treating the eventual (yet not guaranteed) glory as a side effect of my approach to life.

But not this time. This time I was going to appreciate the beauty of the rose petals flung in my path before I trampled them, lol!

With that said, there I was once again hurtling through the air on a transcontinental flight from East to West coast for the 5th Power Summit. That's right folks, count them with me like Tron from Chappelle's show, "One, Two, Three, Four...FIF!" Now think back with me. I sent an innocent innocuous text message to Stephanie back in November

2009, and a mere five in-person encounters later, we were on the verge of giving birth to TPC's first baby...*Sellout!* My success streak remained unbroken!

The fifth meeting really was quite significant. After the 4th Power Summit (where we became an official LLC, built our marketing plan, and really bonded as a group), we went through some very turbulent times. Like they say, tomorrow ain't promised. I could appreciate that sentiment more than ever that day, just as I appreciated Stephanie and James more and more with each week that passed. Through all the good times and tough moments, their work ethic, commitment, faith, and support really inspired me. It is our sincere hope that we have inspired some of you as well.

So enough with the mushy stuff (I love you guys!). Seriously this time, lol. We had another doozy of an agenda on our hands. But there's no rest for the weary over here.

We had a book to launch!

41: The 5th Power Summit
June 11-13, 2010

Only thirteen days out from the eagerly anticipated "blast off," we decided to reunite for one last pre-launch Power Summit. And what a hustle session it was!

First things first... as is tradition, we started the Power Summit with our ritual hike through the redwoods to get our heads right. This time, quite hilariously, we picked up a little homie who, apparently, wanted to be down with TPC.

Dexter the cat (so said his nametag) was awesome. If those nice dog lovers hadn't "rescued" him, we might very well have taken him home with us!

After the hike, we grabbed breakfast, then headed downtown to open the official TPC bank account. As Omar said, you are not officially committed to a company until you transfer large sums of your own cash into the general account. Well, on June 12, 2010, TPC went all in!

We were SO official! ;-)

With that out of the way, the remainder of the Power Summit was spent strategizing about the *Sellout* launch activities. We had lots of planning to do for our official coming out party. We hustled all day and all night, ordering pizza in so we wouldn't have to interrupt our flow. See how we do?

By the time Omar headed back to New Jersey, we had scratched many items off our To-Do list. We finalized the quantities for our initial print-run and developed a variety of promotions for the initial launch. We designed flyers, ads, and posters. We put TPC on LinkedIn and created the Sellout Facebook page. And we filmed more video for the TPC documentary. I'm telling you, the TPC3 be HUSTLIN'!

42: BWRC Here We Come

The TPC3 were frantically preparing for their trip to Atlanta for the BWRC, where we would be launching TPC's debut novel, *Sellout* by James W. Lewis. In six short months we created a vision for a publishing and author services company, implemented that vision, established web presence, obtained LLC status, developed a substantial Facebook fan base, and coordinated the editing and production of our debut novel *Sellout*. Now we headed to Atlanta, with books to sell in hand, a legitimate publishing enterprise.

We worked so hard to get to this moment and it was finally here. We had officially arrived.

There is something very serendipitous about the TPC3 launching James' book at the Black Writer's Reunion and Conference. After all, it was at this conference in July 2006 where the TPC3 crossed paths for the very first time. That fateful weekend, three aspiring authors arrived in Dallas with big dreams and manuscripts to sell.

We didn't come away with book deals, but something even more powerful—lifelong friendships that would eventually serve as the foundation for an ambitious publishing venture—The Pantheon Collective (TPC). It is a testament to the mantra "everything happens for a reason" that these three souls converged at that particular moment in time to form the bond that would set the stage for this momentous occasion. How fitting to bring it all full circle by choosing the BWRC as the site of the official launch.

43: Primetime

James

How does one normally feel the night before the big dance? How does one suppress the emotional avalanche bound to come the moment someone yells "action?" Yeah, you can do all the preparation necessary to hit the stage and perform like a star, but nothing is real until you're actually on that stage and the lights are shining on you.

And that time was finally here.

On Wednesday, June 23, 2010, I was sitting on the couch in our hotel suite (free upgrade!), forced to watch the show *Glee* in my Fruit-of-the-Looms, clothes thrown on just about every cushiony piece of furniture, shopping bags all over the floor like piles of pure madness at my feet. Still, the real madness is within me. Nerves. Fear. Some doubt. Excitement.

You see, the TPC3 would make their grand debut the next day. In the morning I would stand behind a skirted table, all GQ'd out in a blazer and nice jeans, wearing a Kool-Aid smile, pitching my book *Sellout* to customers for the first time. For years I'd attended writer's conferences, watching authors talk about their "babies." I'd always wondered what it would be like to stand behind a table with my own book. Well, as TPC's debut author, I was about to find out.

It was primetime, baby!

44: Sellout *is SO Official*

Omar
June 24, 2010 – Atlanta, GA
W Perimeter Hotel

My stomach churned anxiously as I descended the elevator from the sixth floor to the lobby. It was 9:15 a.m. Walking through the lobby and finding James and Stephanie setting up our booth, I wondered how long it would take for us to make our first sale. Even though it was pretty quiet overall, I had no doubt we would be successful. But I still felt the anxiety I typically experienced just before a big corporate presentation or a big basketball game back in my balling days.

There were only two or three other vendors setting up display tables. I noticed them gazing curiously at us, surely wondering who the author was, or whether the three of us had penned the book together. Ironically, either query would have been met with an affirmative head nod.

Sellout may have James W. Lewis' name on the cover and spine, but it also has the TPC Books logo on there as well. James' rep wasn't the only one on the line here, which probably explained the jagged spike in my heart rate as conference attendees began to pass by—clearly intrigued by the *Sellout* cover, poster, and ultra-dapper author before them.

It's one thing to do the behind the scenes work to bring a book to life; it's quite another to face real-life potential readers. I had to stop myself from overanalyzing their every reaction and tic. Some people engaged the three of us directly. Others read the poster and picked up a flyer. Many picked up the book itself and read the back cover copy—some stoic, others wearing their interest all over their features.

As for the product itself, I was supremely confident. Not only had James written a character-driven, evocative, page-turning novel, but our fans had helped us design the cover and crystallize the back cover copy. So we weren't alone—we were repping the nearly 3,000 collective fans of Stephanie Casher, James Lewis, and Omar Luqmaan-Harris, the real Pantheon Collective!

When all was said and done, 80 percent of the people who stopped by our booth left with a copy of *Sellout* gripped in their possession. Not bad for our soft launch. Along the way, we did a lot of networking, collected a nice amount of cash, signed autographs, conducted interviews, and did quite a bit of celebrating—including a truly epic night out at Opera Club, a local dance joint. A launch that only six weeks before seemed almost certain of not happening (props to Stephanie's superhuman copyediting skills). Once again the Power of Three was able to make the impossible, possible. We're living the dream, and if we can do it, anyone can!

45: Transitions

The TPC3 had officially transitioned from "aspiring authors with a dream" to bonafide publishers! After six months of intense labor to 1) set up the company and 2) prepare our debut novel for printing and distribution, we finally had a product to push! As we moved into this new stage of "selling," we found ourselves facing a whole new set of challenges. How do we most cost-effectively market this book? How do we keep track of sales and manage inventory? And as the orders trickled in, how do we ensure our customers receive the book in a timely manner? Before, we were writers, functioning primarily in isolation as we labored over words on a page. Now, we're out there smiling, schmoozing, and slanging books! 24-7!

And in a few weeks we got to start the cycle all over again when we started production on *When Love Isn't Enough* by Stephanie Casher, which was scheduled for release in Fall 2010. The hustle never stops!

46: Going Postal: From Author to Postman

James
I never thought I'd like going to the post office everyday. Well, I did. I'd gone "postal" up in here—and I was loving it.

We had distribution through Lightning Source, which makes our books available for purchase through online retailers like Amazon and Barnes & Noble. But we also wanted to be able to send autographed copies to readers who preferred a personalized touch, so we kept an inventory on hand, established an account with PayPal for simple transactions, and *boom*! Autographed copy on the way!

The 7x9 envelopes that TPC bought in bulk from Costco (came out to 27 cents per envelope!) fit my book perfectly, like a *Sellout* sleeping bag, nice and snug, the perfect bubble wrap bedding for shipment to any destination. From as close as San Diego to where-the-hell-is-that spots in Australia, I was more than happy to blast off copies of *Sellout* on some international rendezvous courtesy of the postal system.

It felt good. Simple as that. Someone ordering an autographed copy of my firstborn gave me the chilly-willies inside. Smiling all hard, I pulled out my ballpoint pen, autographed the book (careful not to misspell the name or leave out a word), then slapped an adhesive label with the TPC logo on the envelope. Once I "Sharpie" the address and sealed my baby inside, I took my happy butt down to the local USPS and sent the book off to its new home—hopefully to give someone as much joy as it has given me. So damn official!

And I didn't mind standing in long lines at the post office anymore, either. Why? Because I was shipping my pride-and-joy to people who obviously liked what I did from afar. And that's a beautiful thing, for real.

My goal was to be on a first-name basis with every postal worker in the downtown office. I wanted them to greet me with, "Hey, James, how many copies of *Sellout* are we shipping today? Oh, by the way, I loved chapter five!"

47: From Editor to Accountant

Stephanie

Now that TPC had a book that had been edited and printed, and our 3-person street team had hit the ground running, the orders were flowing in. It was a beautiful thing, watching the balance in our PayPal account steadily rise, collecting 10's and 20's from folks who were eager to get their hands on this hot new novel. For me, this was definitely the fun part of this whole experiment, almost worth all those sleepless nights spent in *Sellout* pre-production.

And while I naively thought that I might get a break from the 24/7 hustle as I passed the torch to my sales and marketing team, instead I found that our success required me to don yet *another* hat—the TPC accountant. I mean, somebody had to count the money, right?

In my last job, I was responsible for managing the budgets of two research centers; I am no stranger to crunching numbers. In fact, I'm pretty good at it. So rather than pay an accountant to handle our books, I decided to take it on. Yes, this is another HUGE task to add to my already full plate, but honestly, I just don't trust anyone else to do it. Accounting and bookkeeping are also highly transferable skills, so I figured, what the hell—what I learn now will come in handy for years to come, as TPC is not the only business I plan on starting (have I told y'all about my Editing firm?).

I purchased a copy of QuickBooks and started assembling accounting resources so I could read up on all I needed to know to keep our books clean and manage our bottom line. Man, I had no idea what I was getting into. This accounting stuff is no joke!

Managing TPC's finances was a lot more than just keeping track of sales and expenditures. All income and expenses needed to be categorized for tax purposes; sales tax had to be calculated and paid; shipping costs and PayPal transaction fees needed to be accounted for; inventory needed to be tracked, along with the various price points (retail price vs. friends and family discount vs. book club discount vs. comp copies); royalties needed to be calculated and paid; profit and loss statements generated, as well as cash flow projections; etc, etc. And that's just the tip of the iceberg! There were intricacies in this accounting business I never would have imagined!

With the help of QuickBooks (and the 570-page manual, which I read from cover to cover), I'd successfully set up TPC's chart of accounts and bookkeeping system. Time-consuming, yes, but also incredibly satisfying to have expanded my skill set in such a useful way. TPC was really taking this DIY concept to heart, and every penny we saved on outsourcing we were able to reinvest into making mo' money!

And TPC *loves* money. :)

48: From Marketer to Stalker

Omar

Sit right back / and hear a tale / about a marketing cat / trying to turn fans into sales / he dwells on the web / like 24/7 / persistence and tenacity are his only weapons / imagine his disappointment / when the plan doesn't work out as sketched / but he keeps on pushing / 'cause tomorrow might be the best day yet!

Back when the only stories TPC was slangin' were our own fledgling birth tales, I had a brilliant idea of how we could build our online fan base and virtually guarantee gigantic sales of *Sellout* and the novels to follow. The plan was to put our entire operation on display like the store windows on New York City's 5th Avenue during Christmas. Taking a page out of the Julie/Julia playbook, we would expose our triumphs and tragedies for the entertainment and education of the world.

My next big idea centered around how we could use Facebook as a platform to success. I assumed fans would jump from Facebook to our website and love every minute of the interaction. Once again we saw a rapid initial uptake (mostly friends and family) but then the numbers flattened and stopped growing altogether. As it usually does in these moments, my never say die attitude kicked in and I had yet another genius idea. Because James' book was in the contemporary fiction realm, all we had to do was friend fans of authors who wrote books in the same genre.

Setting a target of 25 new fans a day, we began hitting up total strangers on Facebook. My partners were initially reluctant to try this approach (Stephanie actually never agreed with it), but not me. I dove in head first. Next thing we knew, the fan numbers were climbing again! Going door-to-door was surprisingly successful. Only a handful of people protested my friend request, so I figured it was all good.

I then decided to experiment with Facebook ads. Setting a daily ad budget of $10, I figured I'd let Facebook stalk likely candidates for me. Sure enough, fans began to join our movement in droves! We launched the *Sellout* fan page with another ad and our success continued. I was so bullish on the Facebook strategy by this point that I adjusted our pre-launch sales forecast way up. There was no way we wouldn't easily blow past 1,000 books sold in the first six weeks, right?

Wrong. People may like you on Facebook, and they may even comment on what you're doing every now and again, but asking them to buy something...on Facebook? That's like walking into a busy happy hour and tapping people on the shoulder to ask them to buy a book.

That's when my stalking went into overdrive. I became obsessed with transforming our Facebook fan base into loyal readers, trying everything I could think of to grab people's attention in that crowded bar we call Facebook.

Much love goes out to the early adopters who actually took me up on my many offers. But even more love goes out to those who haven't yet opted in, because all of this stalking is actually making me a better marketer. So I'll be seeing you on a homepage, update, event, or inbox near you. I am a huge proponent of the saying, "If at first you don't succeed, try and try again." So here's to trying!

49: Preparing for My Turn in the Spotlight

Stephanie

Well the past few months have definitely been interesting. Now that we were in full-blown "sell" mode for TPC's debut novel *Sellout*, I had a front-row seat as James was thrust into the limelight. He took the self-promotion component of this hustle very seriously and spent a lot of time reaching out to book clubs and potential readers, interacting with fans, and always, always pushing the product. The level of engagement was high and constant. I'd seen him sell books on airplanes, in restaurants, even at the continental breakfast in our hotel! 'Cause that's what it takes when you're a new author—you have to generate your own buzz. Self-promote, shamelessly.

However, watching him work filled me with a mild anxiety when I thought about the fact that soon it would be MY turn in the spotlight. We had begun pre-production on my novel, *When Love Isn't Enough*, which was scheduled for release in Fall 2010. In addition to the stress I had about meeting the rapidly approaching deadlines for the *When Love Isn't Enough* copyedit and typesetting, I was sincerely dreading all the promotional events and efforts Omar was beginning to line up.

I consider myself an introvert, one of those reclusive writers that would be quite content living in a cabin in the middle of nowhere, writing books and emailing them to my publisher, without ever having to come into contact with the "real world." I'm allergic to schmoozing and thrive in solitude. Don't get me wrong—I'm social when I need to be, but I'm much more comfortable behind the scenes. Unfortunately, if I want my books to SELL, I'm going to have to come out from behind the curtain to meet my public. And soon.

Thankfully, I'd been watching James in action for the past few months, up close and personal, so I had an idea of what to expect. It also helped that we're usually doing promotional events together, which took some of the pressure off because he's more than happy to do most of the talking. ☺ TPC had indeed come a long way in a year's time, with procedures in place and money in the bank; the launch of *When Love Isn't Enough* shouldn't be nearly as stressful as the launch of *Sellout* (fingers crossed). I just hoped my baby received an equally warm reception.

50: Thank You

James

As Biggie once said, "It was all a dream…"

It all started in December 2009—a dream. From imagination to motivation to creation, the three of us jumpstarted our hoopty with the little engine that could and hit the road to publication. Despite the bumps and potholes we anticipated (and ran into), we fully believed we could build upon what little we knew about independent publishing and morph our dreams into something we could hold in our hot little hands. So many routes to take, a thick To-Do list, deadlines to meet... we were living in a freakin' whirlwind. On top of day jobs and school, most of 2010 became a crazy psychedelic haze. Some days, I was like, "Man, can we really do this?"

Well I'm proud to say, *we did it*. All goals met. Edited two manuscripts. Published *Sellout*. Established an online presence. Became an LLC. Attended conferences. Sold books. Published *When Love Isn't Enough*. Sold more books. Got great reviews. Then during the holiday season, chillaxed.

As Stephanie said, we are soooo official. Word.

Yeah, we burned all kinds of fuel trying to get our company in order, but it was worth it. The response to TPC had been phenomenal. Since we debuted *Sellout*, glowing Amazon reviews had been streaming in. As the author, of course I was all geeked out. Eight book clubs made *Sellout* book of the month, and I had four more book club meet-and-greets scheduled for January 2011. The new year wasn't lookin' half-bad.

We released *When Love Isn't Enough* during the holidays, and were off to a great start with our second "child" as well. *When Love Isn't Enough* tapped a whole new market for us because of its tragic love story theme, so the opportunities were endless. I say again, endless. That's where the "No Limits" in the TPC tagline comes in.

We're on an upward trajectory, but we never forget what propels us through the stratosphere—the energy and support from our fans. So thank you! Thank you for buying our books. Thank you for greeting us at conferences. Thank you for friending us on Facebook. Thank you for supporting the TPC3!

Epilogue

The Pantheon Collective (TPC)—Three Years Later

James

Sellout won several independent book awards, including a 2010 Best Book Trailer of the Year from the AALBC and the 2011 Best New Author Award from the National Black Book Festival. Not too shabby for a newbie! My first-born received the kind of love I had hoped for, mostly in the form of four- and five-star reviews. Readers actually loved my book! It might sound a little cliché, but that warm feeling—a kind of we-did-it blanket of pride—I cannot describe in words.

But we couldn't stop with one "child." After releasing *When Love Isn't Enough,* we followed up with my second novel, *A Hard Man is Good to Find,* six months later. *A Hard Man* is an erotic comedy about being careful with what you wish for. With this novel, I wanted to branch out a bit, showing readers I can write drama and comedy with sprinkles of suspense. Because I wrote it in second-person—where the protagonist talks *to* the reader—I knew it would be a novel readers would either love or hate. Luckily, it's been mostly the former, but for the first time, I experienced the dreaded 1-star review (and not the only one). Somebody actually did not like my book! How could that be? Well, hey, that's why authors require skin as thick as crocodiles. Everyone won't love your work. I learned that early. Just brush off the sting (you can't help but feel a little ticked at one-star reviews) and keep it movin'.

TPC published *Sellout* and *A Hard Man*, but as the author, it's been primarily my responsibility to get the word out (as with every author), so I was now promoting two different books. Every author knows writing the book is the easy part; convincing strangers to part from their hard-earned cash is the *real* challenge. But I've been enjoying every minute of it, especially meeting book clubs, conducting interviews (radio, print, and online) and interacting with a social media fan base that grows daily.

Since debuting *A Hard Man*, major seismic tremors in the publishing industry have forced all key players—publishers, literary agents, and authors—to adjust for survival. Borders has closed forever. Amazon is now the number one bookseller in the world. E-books account for 30 percent in total book sales. More people are finding comfort in e-readers. Self-publishing services like LuLu and Amazon's CreateSpace have made it way-too-easy for anyone to publish, which has flooded the market with books of questionable quality—it goes on and on.

How does an indie author stand out?

I stumbled upon a strategy that has been working pretty well for me. Long before I wrote my first novel, I submitted short stories to various online sites, mostly for critique. Realizing I could publish the same stories as e-books on Amazon and other online retailers, I reformatted the stories into e-book format, designed book covers, then uploaded them for either $0.99 or free. It's simple: The more works you have in "rotation," the higher the chances of a potential reader finding and hopefully enjoying your work. I have ten short e-books out right now (I call them "cocktales"). I average about 2000 cocktale downloads a month, about 95 percent of them free downloads. But the best part? Those downloads sometimes lead to sales for my novels, as evidenced by "Customers Who Bought This Also Bought" links.

Despite the industry rumbles, writing is my passion, and I plan to do whatever it takes to roll with the punches, mainly by writing as much as possible. Next up: a new novel titled *Tangled Web*, scheduled to drop in 2014!

Stephanie

After the release of my debut novel, *When Love Isn't Enough,* I held my breath as I waited for the reviews to come in. I experienced the same anxiety that James had, wondering how my book would be received. No one was more surprised than me when the four- and five- star reviews started piling up—*When Love Isn't Enough* was a hit! My debut year was capped off by receiving word that I was one of three finalists for the 2011 Global eBook Award in the Multicultural Fiction category. I didn't end up winning, but believe me, I was beyond honored and proud just to be nominated.

Thanks to the well-oiled TPC promotion machine, my book continued to increase in sales, month after month, with very little promotional effort on my part. Like I said, part of my disengagement with the promotional process is due to my personality (I'm not exactly someone who enjoys the spotlight), but I wasn't exactly available for 'round the clock promotions and social media blitzes because I had to return to the editing cave to work on TPC's next two books, *A Hard Man is Good to Find* and *One Blood*.

The production and release of *A Hard Man is Good to Find* was relatively painless. It was a short book, and in pretty good shape when I got my hands on it. Then I moved on to the edit of *One Blood*. And in between the two, I was freelancing, editing novels for clients and serving as a subcontractor for another editing firm.

As 2011 drew to a close, I found my life had been completely taken over by other people's projects. I was editing nonstop and helping others launch their books, but I wasn't *writing*. And my fan base was pissed—I'd teased that the sequel to *When Love Isn't Enough* would be released in Spring 2012, but I shot waaaay past that deadline. I just didn't have the steam to tackle everything on my plate this time around. I decided to put my book on the back burner so I could dedicate myself to the publication of *One Blood*, which we released in November 2011.

After the hustle heavy 2010 (The Year of TPC) and an exhausting 2011 (The Year of the Other), I was ready to anoint 2012 the Year of ME. And that's exactly what I did. I took an editing sabbatical and turned away paying clients so I could work on my own novel. I withdrew from the time suck that is social media. I informed my partners that I was on hiatus from TPC business, and that they were going to have to promote and market *One Blood* without my assistance. Anything that even remotely felt like an "obligation" was relegated to the back burner.

With my priorities reordered, I was finally able to carve out space to write and got 3/4 of the way through my new novel, *The Space Between*. A large portion of this novel is set in Europe, and I felt it was my duty, in order to write authentically about this setting, for me to actually travel there for research. So in September 2012, that's exactly what I did—jetted off to Europe solo diva style for 11 days of adventure. It was an incredible experience, and my novel is so much better because of it.

I look forward to finally completing and releasing the long-awaited next installment of the *Soul Mates Trilogy*. My fans have been beyond patient, and it's time to make them a priority as well.

Omar

After successfully launching three books into the publishing pantheon, in November 2011, it was finally my turn. I had a lot of best practices under my belt. I had two years of learning how to build an audience and get my book found one reader at a time. I had a very clear vision for how it was going to go—but as the saying goes, "Man plans, God laughs." I came into 2012 ready to make a name for myself and my little book, *One Blood*. By the end of the year, I had exceeded even my most audacious expectations.

One Blood started off with a bang, garnering five-star review after five-star review from casual readers, bloggers, friends, and family. The sales were much slower to follow, but they steadily increased as the year matured. In February 2012, The Kirkus Book Review, known as some of the toughest book critics around, named *One Blood* as a novel of remarkable merit—awarding it the glorious Kirkus star. In March and April, *One Blood* officially became a bestseller, making the AALBC Best Sellers list twice in that period.

Spring melted into summer and then the awards came. Readers, industry big wigs, and authors in attendance at The Book Expo America Conference in June, heard my name called at the Jacob Javits Center in conjunction with the Indie Reader Discovery Awards, where *One Blood* not only won its category, but was judged as the 2nd best fiction novel overall! I got to hobnob with other authors at the Plaza Hotel in New York for the Next Generation Indie Book Award's ceremony. I picked up two International Book awards in July, and a global eBook Award in August.

By this time, thousands of readers had clicked the "Buy" link on Amazon.com. It was all happening so fast, yet I was still unsatisfied. I wanted to go bigger. So I started reaching out to literary agents in the hope that I could enter into a hybrid deal with them around *One Blood* where they would own the print rights to the book and TPC would retain the digital rights. Due to the success of the book, the agents were very amenable to receiving a copy. Then the rejections started pouring back in just when I thought I was done with rejection. Guess not.

As 2012 drew to a close, I accepted a job that would take me out of NY and fling me halfway around the world to Istanbul, Turkey in the beginning of December. By this time, *One Blood* had already been downloaded over 10,000 times on Amazon and my stock was still rising. I partnered with Wattpad in October and received another 440,000 reads of *One Blood* as a result. And then Kirkus came calling again, this time to let me know that *One Blood* had made their prestigious Best of List for 2012!

A few other highlights for me from 2012 were launching my author website, qwantuamaru.com, crossing the 2,000 fan mark on my *One Blood* Facebook fan page, speaking to 70 or so 6th graders about writing in October, and launching my book marketing site, AuthorDiscovery.com. I ended the year making the AALBC 2012 Bestsellers list (#11 and #18 e-book/print book respectively), as well as the MosaicBooks. com bestsellers list (#6)!

2014 and Beyond...

It's amazing what 48 months can do.

It can transform three writers and aspiring authors into publishing partners. It can transform three writers into published authors. It can create a loyal fan base some 12,000 people strong. It can test and challenge even the strongest of bonds—be it kindred spirits or romantic partners. It can be filled with triumphs and troughs more exhilarating and terrifying than the fastest, tallest, "twistiest" roller coaster. It can make you or break you.

Well, here we are, the TPC3, still standing four years later. This is definitely a moment for quiet reflection and raucous celebration. We have to thank all you supporters out there who have buoyed us with your words, energy, hard earned cash, reviews, recommendations, and active presence. We would not be here were it not for all of you.

Omar was running the numbers recently and came up with a pretty impressive statistic. In the 30 months since *Sellout* was launched, our fledgling independent publishing venture has sold over 25,000 copies combined of our four novels, *Sellout*, *When Love Isn't Enough*, *A Hard Man is Good to Find*, and *One Blood*! Selling 25,000 copies is not going to keep any of the Big 6 publishers awake at night worried about us, but it is a significant achievement nonetheless.

Did you know that most independently published books sell less than 500 copies in their lifetime? When you look at it that way you can see why we are so excited! And with the launch of this book as well as all the big things we have planned for 2014, it truly is onward and upward for the TPC3.

As James noted, the industry has changed a lot in the three years since we launched *Sellout*. Not only did Borders go bankrupt and Barnes & Noble closed thousands of stores, but the Big 6 traditional publishers have become the "Bigger 5" with the merger of Random House and Penguin. Amazon has even extended their digital dominance with KDP Select, Amazon prime, and the recent acquisition of social reading site, Goodreads.

We enter our fifth year more experienced and much wiser in the ways of this publishing world, but we will still need a lot of energy for the next phase of our journey. In 2014 we plan to publish Stephanie Casher's 2nd novel, *The Space Between*, develop a "how-to" primer on starting an independent publishing venture for aspiring authorpreneurs (tentatively titled *The Independent Publishing Plan),* and launch our unique take on author services. All three partners are also hard at work on new novels, in addition to attending conferences, conducting bookstore, radio, and blog tours, interacting with book clubs, and continuing our blog. As the times and technologies change, TPC remains committed to staying on top of the trends and helping others navigate this ever-changing publishing landscape. As far as we've come and as much as we've grown, we still remain committed to our original mission to empower and inspire.

In other words—we're just getting started.

About the Authors

Stephanie Casher is a freelance editor and author of multicultural women's fiction. Her debut novel, *When Love Isn't Enough*, has received 4- and 5- star reviews on amazon.com, and was a finalist in the 2011 Global eBook Awards for Multicultural Fiction. The sequel, *The Space Between*, will be released in 2014. Currently living in Santa Cruz, California, she travels extensively in search of inspiration.

James W. Lewis is an award-winning novelist and freelance writer published in several books that include *Chicken Soup for the Soul* (two series), *Gumbo for the Soul, Truth Be Told: Tales of Life, Love and Drama, Don't Forget your Pepper Spray* and New York Times best-selling author Zane's anthology *Caramel Flava*. As a managing partner of the publishing company The Pantheon Collective, he published his two novels, the award-winning *Sellout* and *A Hard Man is Good to Find*.

After spending twenty years in the Navy, James retired from active duty and is now completing graduate studies in Exercise Physiology. In addition to writing and physical fitness, he loves to deejay and has a collection of over 300 vinyl records. He also does extensive volunteer work at a local veterans assistance center.

Omar Luqmaan-Harris (aka Qwantu Amaru) has been writing poetry, stories, and novels under the pen name Qwantu Amaru (kwan-too a-mar-oo) since 1998. In his day job, he currently works for Big Pharma in Istanbul, Turkey, while researching and writing Qwantu Amaru's next thriller, *The Uneasy Sleep of Giants*. For more information on Omar and Qwantu, check out authordiscovery.com, the website he created to help more authors get discovered by their readers.

Titles available from

The Pantheon Collective

(TPC Books)

TPC
BOOKS

For ordering information visit:
www.pantheoncollective.com

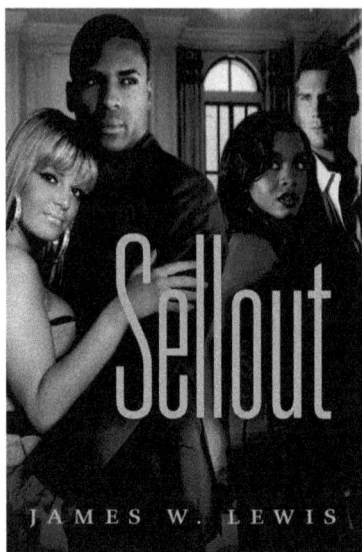

Sellout by James W. Lewis

People who date interracially are often called traitors to their own kind. Self-haters. Sellouts.

Loan Officer Tammy McDonald has just come out of another failed relationship with a wannabe thug. To break this destructive pattern, she leaves her home city of Dallas for San Diego. As she settles in rainbow California, fantasies of meeting an ebony prince fade, so she eyes Dale Bristol as a potential ivory replacement.

Terrell Jackson is San Diego's only black optometrist. Women regularly drop in for more than just eye exams, but he stays true to his girl, Tasha, until a wet dream unleashes a ridiculous outburst. Fed up with her jealous fits, he denounces the common "dedramanators" in his life—black women.

Even though Penelope Miller was raised in the South by a racist father once affiliated with the KKK, she can't ignore her attraction to black men. But she never expected to fall in love with one...nor did she expect her "interracial felony" to threaten their lives.

Sellout follows these three individuals and the consequences of dating outside their race. In the quest to find what they think is missing in their lives, they encounter guilt, fear, and mess they never anticipated... including murder.

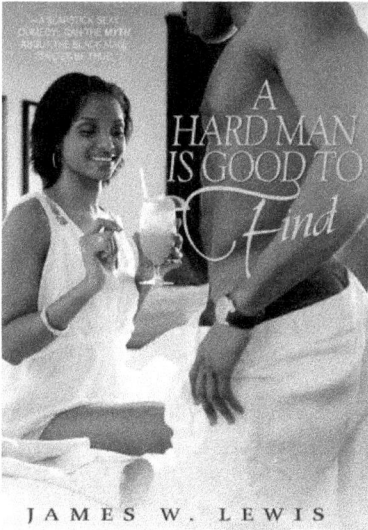

A Hard Man is Good to Find
by James W. Lewis

MICHELLE LARSEN has found a man straight out of a romance novel—handsome, fit, educated, and pulling in a six-figure income. Despite the exceptional qualities and his obvious interest in her, things are moving too slow between them. Unlike most men who can't wait to get in her pants, this particular man refuses to take things to the next level.

DARYL JACKSON has grown tired of the nightclub scene and wants to settle down, but he has a secret that always seems to interrupt any potential love connection once he reveals it. He believes Michelle is the ideal woman, but can she handle the truth?

After six weeks of dating, and still no attempt from him to get her "horizontal," Michelle grows sex-starved. She is driving herself crazy trying to figure out Daryl's problem! During a weekend getaway in Palm Springs, Michelle finally puts an end to the what's-wrong-with-Daryl guessing game and demands to know what's up. Not only does Daryl answer all her questions, Michelle learns first hand that you really need to be careful with what you wish for!

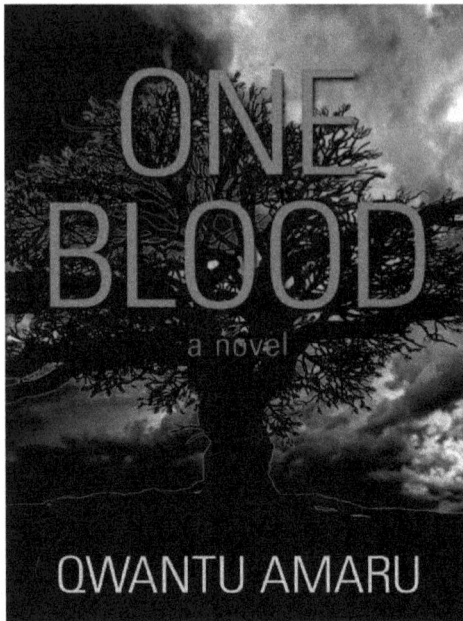

One Blood
by Qwantu Amaru

One Blood is a supernatural thriller that will leave you wanting more from this author. Rich themes of voodoo, family curses, political ambitions, and a quest for power are dominant in this roller coaster ride set in Louisiana. Governor Randy Lafitte is popular and beloved after battling back from brain cancer, but his political success has come at a price. When his daughter is kidnapped, Lafitte is confronted with a past he thought died a long time ago. However, what hasn't caught you, hasn't passed you. And what comes for Lafitte may be way more than he or the forces behind him can handle as he fights the demons (literally demons) from his past.

*(The first book in the **Soul Mates** Trilogy)*

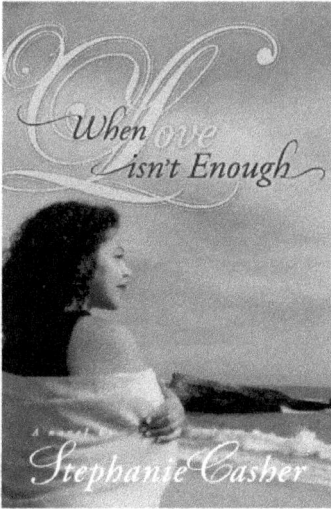

<u>When Love Isn't Enough</u>
<u>by Stephanie Casher</u>

Samantha's second year of college started with heartbreak and betrayal. Lost and lonely, she'd completely given up on ever finding love again when a chance encounter put her in contact with the man who would change her life.

Tony never believed in love at first sight—until he laid eyes on Samantha. But within moments of meeting her, he knew without a doubt that she was the woman he was put on this earth to love. There was only one problem—Angela, his girlfriend of five years.

Tony doesn't want to hurt Angela, with whom he shares a rich history, but his connection to Samantha is undeniable. Angela, however, is not about to let the love of her life go without a fight.

When desperation takes a tragic turn, a chain of events unfolds that changes the course of all three of their lives forever. It is a heartbreaking tale of true love, terrible timing, impossible choices, and how you find the strength to go on when you discover that, sometimes, love just isn't enough...

*The series continues with **The Space Between**, available in 2014.*

There's who you are…Who you were…
And then there's

The Space Between

Available in 2014!

From the terrace of my hotel suite, I stared down at the collection of people gathered to witness our nuptials. It was a small ceremony, nothing fancy, with only our nearest and dearest in attendance. In a few minutes, it would be time to head down to the beach, in my strapless white gown, to become Mrs. Damion Waters.

Panic gripped my rapidly beating heart. *I don't think I can go through with this.*

Not because I didn't love him—I loved Damion with all my heart. He was my *best* friend, a truly amazing man. I'd never had someone so devoted to my care and comfort. But that spark, that out of control, life-consuming fire—it just wasn't there. I'd tried to convince myself that a steady, solid, reliable love was more important than passion, but after the events of last month, I had come face to face with the fact that I was kidding myself. Settling. Maybe if I'd never known that kind of passion, I wouldn't miss it so much. But I knew what it felt like to love someone so much you could barely breathe, and no matter how hard I tried, I couldn't forget.

Damn you, Tony. Damn you, damn you, damn you.

My sister, Megan, came up behind me, resting her hand on the small of my back. "You about ready?" she asked.

I set my bouquet of calla lilies on the table. "Can you get Damion for me?"

"Isn't it bad luck for the groom to see the bride before the wedding?"

"Meg, I don't think there's going to be a wedding…"

Chapter One
Samantha

I've tried really hard to live my life with honor and integrity, especially when it comes to matters of the heart. After all, the heart is a fragile thing, the seat of human vulnerability, our Achilles heel. A major break can do irreparable damage, and I'm speaking from experience on this one, having lived through the after effects of an all-consuming, life-wrecking love affair.

When I was nineteen years old, I met the man who I believed to be my soulmate. We had that magical chemistry you see in movies; the moment we laid eyes on each other for the first time, we just *knew*. Up to that point, I was somewhat of a cynic—my first "love" had ended in heartbreak and completely damaged my ability to trust. But the connection I shared with Tony, said soulmate, was not something I could deny. And believe me, I tried. There are just some people who, once they get hooks into your heart, are impossible to shake.

Yes, it's always exciting to meet the man of your dreams, and discovering he returns your feelings is all kinds of euphoric. Fate at work. But Tony came with a rather significant complication—a girlfriend. A girlfriend who, for reasons I still struggle to understand, he found it difficult to sever ties with. Tony, bless his non-confrontational, peace-loving heart, couldn't stand the thought of hurting anyone. As Damion used to say, this was Tony's best and worst quality.

###

Damion—a tall, dark, dreadlocked Adonis—was Tony's best friend. When we met, Damion was in his fourth year as a graduate student in the History of Consciousness Ph.D program at UC Santa Cruz, where we all went to school. Damion is one of those impossibly smart, activist-oriented, hip-hop intellectuals; his insightful critiques of the establishment were reminiscent of KRS-One and Public Enemy. Heavily influenced by the psychologist Frantz Fanon, he double-majored in History and Psychology at the University of Oregon and was now writing his dissertation on the psychology of the oppressed and the absence of contemporary social movements in the United States.

Damion's greatest passion was the empowerment of underrepresented minorities in underserved communities, and he was committed to using his voice to speak out against all forms of injustice. An accomplished orator and professional keynote/emcee, he could frequently be found onstage at some event, mic in hand, trying to incite the next revolution. He never passed up an opportunity to drop knowledge and wisdom on impressionable, young minds. Possessing hypnotic charisma, Damion would open his mouth and audiences would fall in rapture. To this day, I've never met someone with greater powers of persuasion.

Damion also gave awesome hugs, which I took advantage of on many occasions while I waited for Tony to figure things out. When Tony finally managed to free himself from his relationship with Angela, we embarked on what was supposed to be a long and passionate journey together. But Angela had other plans. A series of tragic events drove a wedge between Tony and I, turning us into star-crossed lovers. Convinced that we were destined to be together, I put my life on hold and waited for him… refusing to give up on the future we had planned.

During our estrangement, Tony and I did most of our communicating through Damion, and Damion provided a strong, supportive shoulder for me to cry on during those long, hard months. Honestly, I don't know if I would have made it through that phase of my life without Dame. During the lowest of the lows, he was a true friend, and over time, I came to rely on him.

Tony never made it back to me, and I was left devastated and heartbroken. I truly believed he was *The One*; it never occurred to me that there were forces in this world strong enough to keep soulmates apart. That maybe true love *couldn't* conquer all. I don't know what was more tragic— losing Tony, or losing the part of me that still believed in true love and the possibility of happily ever after.

In the wake of Tony's abandonment, Damion and I built upon our budding friendship. My wounds were still pretty raw, deep lacerations that refused to scab over. To guard against infection, I decided to keep people, men especially, at a distance. I was determined to protect myself by any means necessary. But for some reason, my defense mechanisms never kicked in when Damion was around. I've always felt completely safe with him, and his tender, loving care played a huge part in my healing.

Damion was also a fantastic influence on me scholastically. While I worked toward my BA in Sociology, Damion was finishing up his dissertation and trying to line up a job in preparation for his inevitable entry into the real world. He was so focused and driven, quite the contrast to my peers who were more interested in partying than planning for the future. I found myself emulating his work ethic and attitude towards academics, and earned straight-A's my junior and senior years.

We never spoke about Tony. Of course I was curious, but I knew better than to open that door again. Tony had made his choice (if you could even call it a choice), and I had vowed not to waste another moment with my life on hold. There had been enough of that nonsense.

Somewhere along the way, Damion developed a crush on me, which we came very close to acting on while I was rebounding from Tony. But deep down, I knew it was wrong. Not only were Tony and Damion like brothers, but I was in no position to return Damion's feelings. Damion had been such a good friend to me; it wasn't right to use him as a distraction. Which is all he could have been because I was still very much in love with his best friend.

Damion was the perfect gentleman and never pressed the issue, appearing content with the platonic bond we'd forged. I'd see him once or twice a week and we'd go hiking, to the movies, or catch a show downtown at the Catalyst. I actually credit him with bringing the fun back into my world after a long bout of depression and hibernation.

"Come on," he said, dragging me towards the Rock-O-Plane, one of his favorite rides at the Santa Cruz Beach Boardwalk. "We have time for one more ride before the show starts."

Steel cages dangled from the limbs of the ferris wheel towering above us. "I don't know, Dame. That might be a little too much spinning for my current state of intoxication."

"Oh, you'll be fine," he said.

He was always saying that, "you'll be fine." Right before he nudged (or shoved) me outside of my comfort zone.

"Alright, but if I puke all over your Jordans, it's on you. Literally."

I managed to keep the contents of my stomach where they belonged, and after a laughter-filled spin on the Rock-O-Plane, we headed down to the beach for the show. Every Friday night the Boardwalk hosted a free concert on the beach, and the line-up was great for the nostalgia factor. So far we'd seen Eddie Money, the Family Stone (minus Sly), and the Gin Blossoms. Tonight's entertainment would be provided by 90's pop queen, Tiffany.

We had a blast drinking beer and singing along to her cheesy (but classic) tunes like "I Think We're Alone Now," a song I hadn't heard in years, yet still knew *every word*. To my amusement, I discovered Damion knew every word as well. That was one of the lovely paradoxes about Damion—while he was smart, studious and articulate enough to hold his own in a debate with Cornel West, he was still able to access his inner ten-year-old with ease. The man could put in work, but also knew how to play, as accomplished in the art of silliness as any other subject.

As my Junior year drew to a close, Damion successfully defended his dissertation and was preparing to head to London. He'd been offered a postdoctoral fellowship at Goldsmiths University, where he planned to conduct research for a comparative study on US and UK youth uprisings. This was an amazing opportunity for him, and I shared his excitement. But as his departure date drew near, the magnitude of what this meant for our friendship began to sink in. Damion, my faithful companion and BFF, was moving to *London*.

A week before his departure, we took one final trek into the Pogonip, a heavily forested state park adjacent to the UCSC campus. Our ritual was to hike deep into the forest and pause for a smoke break underneath our favorite tree, Papa Wood. In the book, *The Celestine Prophecy,* James Redfield claimed that old-growth redwoods were a critical source of energy that people could tap into to increase their own personal reserves. Papa Wood, whose trunk was easily twelve feet in diameter, definitely fell into the "old-growth" category and we'd spent many afternoons with our backs against his sturdy trunk, meditating on the mysteries of life.

Damion took a seat and passed me his palm-sized glass pipe, the bowl packed with Santa Cruz's finest tasty greens. I took a hit and passed the pipe back to him, a stream of smoke passing over my lips as I exhaled.

"I can't believe this is our last session under this tree," Damion said.

"Don't remind me." I was enjoying my bubble of denial about Damion's departure, not yet ready for the inevitable burst.

"I don't think they have redwood forests in England," he mused. "I wonder what I'll do when I need to replenish my energy. I've been spoiled living in Santa Cruz so long. Folks are of a very high spiritual caliber here."

"If there are spiritual folks to be found, I have no doubt you will draw them to you. You're a magnet when it comes to that stuff." And it was the truth. Damion was a living, breathing poster child for the Law of Attraction—he put peaceful, positive vibes out into the Universe on a regular basis and was continuously blessed with opportunity and good fortune. I truly believed my life had been improved by sheer proximity, and was mildly concerned that his departure would trigger a depressive doom spiral.

"Won't be the same without my wing woman," he said with a wink.

"Maybe now you'll be able to find yourself a lady friend who can offer more perks than companionship," I teased.

Damion grew quiet, his brows bending toward the center of his face. "Still won't be the same."

I'd tried many times to encourage Damion to take a dip in the dating pool, but he always had an excuse handy:

"These days, dating and drama go hand in hand. Who's got time for that?"

"A girlfriend will just distract me from the work I need to do on my dissertation."

"It doesn't make sense to start a relationship right now—I'm getting ready to leave the country."

And so on. While those were all valid points, I always suspected there was more to it, like he was still carrying a torch for me. Which is why I frequently tried to direct his affection elsewhere. But now that his attention was about to be permanently reassigned as he was physically removed from my sphere, separation anxiety was setting in. The more I contemplated 'Life without Damion,' the more I realized how attached I'd become over the past year. Without any drama or complications, we'd been fulfilling each other's need for companionship and emotional connection. His absence was going to create a huge void in my life, and I was starting to freak out. Isn't that the way it always is though? You never realize how much something means to you until you're on the verge of losing it…

Chapter Two
Samantha

Damion's last night in Santa Cruz was very emotional. I dread goodbyes—they always bring me back to the day Tony left. But this one was particularly hard because the person I usually turned to for comfort and support was the one leaving.

Damion was a beloved member of the UCSC community, and his going-away party was festive and well-attended by students and faculty alike. His mother even flew in from Los Angeles, and it was wonderful to see her again. I had met Damion's mother for the first time when Damion had taken me down to LA for my final showdown with Tony. It was during this trip that I realized a future with Tony was no longer a possibility, and Mama Waters (as she is affectionately known) was a great comfort to me, even though Tony is like a son to her.

As I sat on the porch that July night, Mama Waters sat down beside me with a pot of chamomile tea. I clutched the warm mug between my palms, holding on for dear life. My tears hadn't stopped flowing since Tony drove away; I was inconsolable.

Damion had been a wonderful support, driving me down to LA for the confrontation against his better judgment, but I'll never forget how comforting it was to have the company and counsel of another woman at that moment of intense fragility. I didn't share the details of my plight with her, but for some reason I sensed that Mama Waters understood the depth of my agony, the severity of my wound. She didn't press, preach or judge. In fact, she barely spoke at all, except to impart these timeless words of wisdom:

"Things don't always turn out like we planned, and that's okay. You have to trust that there's a bigger plan at work. We are always being prepared for something better, or protected from something worse." She patted my hand. "We may not see it at the time, but I promise you, it's true."

I held onto those words as my mantra during my darkest days.

Her outlook on life was remarkable considering all she'd been through. Mama Waters was the epitome of grace under pressure. She had raised Damion as a single mother in one of the roughest neighborhoods in South Central LA, where the life expectancy of black males was painfully short. She experienced this firsthand when her firstborn son, Khalil, was gunned down in a gang-related shooting a few months before his 16th birthday. Determined to save Damion from a similar fate, she worked two jobs to earn enough money to move them to a safer neighborhood in a better school district. Damion was all she had left and she would not let him become a statistic.

Mama Waters hadn't walked the easiest of roads, but the years of struggle made moments like this all the more poignant. Damion, her baby boy, had beat the odds. He was now the recipient of a Ph.D., *Doctor* Damion Waters. Not bad for a boy from the hood. But what was truly impressive is that he was just getting started. Damion's idealism and activist bent were the real deal—he was determined to make a difference in this world. He wasn't content to settle on a career, he wanted to build a *legacy*.

Every guest at Damion's going away party that offered a toast (and there were many of them) spoke of how Damion had changed their life. Helped them see something in a different light. Damion had inherited his mother's positive outlook, and had a calming effect on people. The ability to bring peace to others with his mere presence was Damion's special gift, one that was much appreciated since there was no shortage of people out there doing thoughtless, fucked up shit to each other. But not Damion. He made everything better, and asked for very little in return. Which only made him more beloved.

Mama Waters stood proudly in the corner as love and appreciation was showered upon her son. The speeches went on and on until Damion refocused the love in his mother's direction, giving credit where credit was due. We were all holding back tears as he expressed his love and admiration for his mother, clearly the driving force behind every ounce of greatness he aspired to.

"This woman," Damion proclaimed as his mom tried to shake the blush from her cheeks. "She sacrificed so much, every step of the way, so that I could have access to opportunities for a better life. The greatest gift you can give your kids is the chance to chase their dreams. I'm a project kid; I'm not supposed to be here, with fancy letters after my name, poised to wield actual power against the establishment. And I wouldn't be here, without the love, support and guidance of this incredible woman, my mother, Mrs. Corrine Waters.

"Ma, thank you for all you sacrificed for me to get here. For putting a roof over my head and putting me through college. For always putting me first. For teaching me that there is nobility in selflessness. I do this all for, and because of, you."

The room erupted in applause. Raising a man of that caliber is no small feat, and we all owed Mrs. Waters a tremendous debt of gratitude.

Damion stopped by my house before he hit the road, his last stop before bidding farewell to the Cruz. I admit, I was tempted not to answer the door, hoping Damion would refuse to leave town if I denied him the opportunity to say a proper goodbye. I'd never experienced such severe separation anxiety, not even with Tony. It could be years before we saw each other again, and the reality of what that meant was finally starting to hit me.

I know, codependent, much?

"London's just so *far*, you know?" I pouted.

"It is," he said. "But think of it this way—now you have somewhere to stay if you ever decide to visit Europe."

"I may just take you up on that. A flight to London sounds like a great graduation present." I forced a smile.

Having something to look forward to, no matter how impractical, made parting a bit easier.

As he pulled me into an embrace, I tried not to think about how this was our *last* hug. But my emotions eventually got the best of me as tears escaped my eyes and hurried down my cheeks to soak the sleeve of his shirt.

"I'm going to miss you so much," I whispered. "You're one of the best friends I've ever had."

Damion stepped back and wiped the tears away with his thumb. "No matter where I am in this world, I will *always* have your back. But you're going to be fine." He planted a kiss on my cheek. "You're a lot stronger than you think."

I wasn't feeling particularly strong at the moment, but I *wanted* to be the brave woman Damion saw when he looked at me. Was I really ready to stand on my own two feet, with no crutches or shoulders to lean on?

I was about to find out.

Chapter Three
Damion

Samantha will never know how close I came to *not* boarding that flight to London.

When I felt the first trace of moisture on her cheek, I was done. What was I doing? Was I really trying to be an ocean away from the woman I loved? It didn't make any damn sense.

Not that she knew I loved her. No, that just would have made things awkward as she mourned the loss of the love of her life, my best friend, Tony Carteris.

Fucking Tony. He had really messed this one up—for all of us. If he had done right by Samantha the first time around, I never would have been put in this position. Tony saw her first, and loved her first, and would have had my full support in riding off into the proverbial sunset with this amazing girl. But for some reason, he had the hardest time manning up and handling his business, i.e. Angela.

That girl. The anti-Samantha. Selfish, conniving, a professional victim. She had Tony twisted up in knots of guilt and obligation and it just wasn't right. The two of them were trapped in a toxic, dysfunctional relationship, the most miserable existence. I'll never understand why Tony chose to forgo light and true love for something dark and seeped in despair.

After Tony broke up with Samantha (in the coldest, cruelest way possible), he asked me to look after her. Make sure she was alright. In Tony's defense, he did truly believe that pushing Samantha away so she could move on and find happiness was in her best interests. But deep down, he knew he'd done a fucked up thing and caused Samantha unnecessary pain. I guess he figured anointing her personal protector would ease some of his guilt. How was he, or I, supposed to know I'd end up falling for her, too?

Samantha is an easy person to love. Smart and beautiful, compassionate and kind, she possessed the emotional fortitude of someone twice her age. My attraction to her was instantaneous, and while I tried and tried to fight it, the feelings only grew as time wore on.

As you can imagine, Tony was *not* happy when he learned about my little crush. Yes, I violated guy code by falling for my best friend's girl, but it's not like I acted on it. Even if I wanted to, there was no room for me in Samantha's heart—she was in love with my best friend.

She's *still* in love with my best friend.

I'm not big on unrequited love, so fleeing to Europe seemed like a great way to keep the situation from escalating. I had received fellowship offers from both Cornell University and UCLA, but Goldsmiths in London was the one that served dual purposes. Not only would I be able to conduct ethnographic research in a country with a long history of civil unrest, but 5500 miles was exactly the kind of distance I needed to get control of my feelings and try, as futile as those attempts may be, to get over Samantha.